英文

日本絵とき事典

ILLUSTRATED

JAPANESE FAMILY & CULTURE

［日本の家族］

D1572187

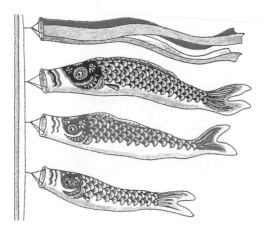

ILLUSTRATED
JAPANESE FAMILY & CULTURE

1st edition **1994**
6th edition **2003**

Printed in Japan

About this Book

1) Layout
   This book consists of the following seven sections (1) From Birth
to Old Age (2) Everyday Life (3) Festivities Throughout the Year (4)
Traditional and Modern Culture (5) From the Stone Age to the Age
of Affluence(6) Family Problems.

2) Japanese Words
   All the Japanese words in this book have been romanized in
accordance with the revised Hepburn system. Except for the names
of places and people, all Japanese words are printed in italics except
where they appear in headings or bold type. Long vowels are indicated by a line above, as in *'Shintō'*; and, since e's are pronounced
"ay" in Japanese, e's at the ends of words are marked with an acute
accent, as in *'saké'* (pronounced "sakay").

Dear Readers

●

Years ago the Japanese were sometimes characterized as "inscrutable." But the lives of ordinary Japanese are not hard to fathom.

This book allows you to enter a Japanese home, where you can look at everyday family life from the inside. You will see how family members cope with the stress of modern living. Illustrations of special events, such as festivals, weddings and funerals, will lead you into the personal lives and thoughts of the Japanese. Life in Japan is, like anywhere else, a mixture of mundane existence and exotic ceremony.

Japanese families and individuals make up an all-encompassing "family," the nation of Japan, with its long and unique culture. Illustrations of Japan through the centuries, from the Stone Age through the period of medieval strife to the modern age of affluence, will show you a different side of this complex yet hardly inscrutable country.

CONTENTS

Chapter 1 FROM BIRTH TO OLD AGE
第1章　家族の一生

Chapter 2 EVERYDAY LIFE
第2章　家族の生活

Chapter 3　FESTIVITIES THROUGHOUT THE YEAR
第3章　家族の四季

Chapter 4 TRADITIONAL AND MODERN CULTURE
第 4 章 外国の人を招く

Chapter 5　FROM THE STONE AGE TO THE AGE OF AFFLUENCE
第5章　家族の変遷

Chapter 6　FAMILY PROBLEMS
第6章　家族の問題

COLUMN

FROM BIRTH TO OLD AGE
家族の一生

DIFFERENT LIFESTYLES FOR DIFFERENT FOLKS

日本の家族形態のいろいろ

Years ago most Japanese assumed that their family lineage would continue uninterrupted from the distant past into the distant future. Aging parents expected their eldest son to live with them, along with his wife and children. But now cities have mushroomed and women want to work, so things are vastly different now.

The Nuclear Family

The modern stereotype, often a reality, has husband and wife crammed into a small, unattractive apartment (derisively called a 'rabbit hutch') in a big city with their off-spring, with no space at all for aging parents. (See page 178.)

Three Generations under One Roof

Before World War II Japanese households were typified as a married couple and their children, sharing a home with either the husband's or the wife's parents. Recently this model (or at least two generations living together—see page 179) is being viewed favorably again, especially because of tremendously high land prices in large cities.

DINKS

A great number of women now want a social position outside the home as well, and some have no interest in raising children. This has led to Double Income, No Kids.

DEWKS

DINKS has gone one step further—have it all as Dual Employed With Kid, and share all the housework and child rearing too.

One Parent with Grown Children

Everybody has to pick up the pieces after a divorce or the death of a spouse. One solution is to move in with a grown child. And in some cases the wife has this option too when her husband is posted far from home.

Empty Nesters

Children leave and aging parents are left on their own. But some elderly are all too glad to say good-bye to the youngsters, in order to spend their remaining years as they wish.

The Solitary Oldster

After divorce or the death of a spouse some elderly end up living alone. Some landlords refuse to rent to oldsters who choose, or are forced, to live alone.

The Japanese language is rich in words that are chosen according to the situation or the person being spoken to. The less intimate the circle, the more formal (and, generally, humble) the language (though some teen-agers somehow can't be bothered with such formalities).

◆ Words for "Father" and "Mother"

O-tōsan, o-kāsan

Commonly used. After a couple has a child they may use these same words for each other, rather than say the spouse's name.

O-tōchan, o-kāchan

Childish endearments replacing o-tōsan, o-kāsan.

O-tōsama, o-kāsama

Very polite form. Usually used when talking with others, referring to their parents as a sign of respect.

Papa, mama

Children have picked up these anglicisms. Adults might use them too, though would perhaps be uncomfortable if they were overheard by outsiders.

Chichi, haha, ryōshin

When talking about one's parents, or introducing them to others. Ryōshin literally means "both parents."

Oyaji, ofukuro

Only used by males in their teens or older, to refer to their own parents. Hardly genteel.

◆ Words for "Husband" and "Wife"

Shujin, otto, nyōbō, kami-san, yomé-san

When speaking to others about one's spouse.

Husbands use the wife's personal name, or the somewhat abrupt *omaé*, or, when calling, an even abrupter *oi!* Wives likewise say the husband's name, or *anata* (often shortened as time goes on to a word that sounds rather perfunctory, *anta*).

Yadoroku, gusai

To show humility Japanese people might appear to demean their spouse, though their true feelings are assumed to be quite different. (The *'gu'* of *gusai* means dull-witted; *'sai'* means wife.)

◆ Words for "Grandfather" and "Grandmother"

O-jii-chan, o-bā-chan

These words, used by grandchildren too, express a feeling of fondness and intimacy.

O-jii-san, o-bā-san

Most commonly used words. Also used when addressing older people one is not even related to.

Sofu, sobo

Used in formal situations.

GETTING MARRIED

結婚 ＜家族の始まり＞

Since World War II Japanese society has generally thought of the married couple as the basic unit of the family. Marriage is thus the creation of a new family.

The following is a description of a typical engagement and wedding.

Engagement Presents

The engagement is formalized with a ceremonial exchange of presents. The go-betweens (*nakōdo*) arrive at the fiancee's home with nine items from the young man, many of which are symbolic.

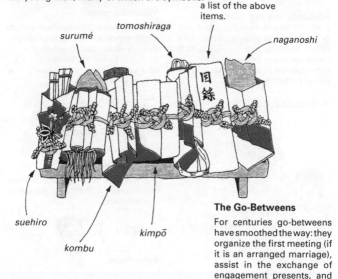

a list of the above items.

surumé

tomoshiraga

naganoshi

suehiro

kombu

kimpō

Seven of the ceremonial betrothal gifts from the man:

The Go-Betweens

For centuries go-betweens have smoothed the way: they organize the first meeting (if it is an arranged marriage), assist in the exchange of engagement presents, and play an important role at the wedding ceremony.

The Wedding Ceremony

Tying the knot ceremonially is done at a Shinto shrine, a Christian church, or a Buddhist temple. Nowadays often the religious ceremony is done at the wedding hall, just before the reception, as a perfunctory acceptance of form.

The small, medium-sized and large cups are each brought to the lips three times, one sip each time. (*San-san-ku* means 3 X 3 = 9.)

San-san-ku-do

If at a shrine, the bride and groom recite their marriage vows to the god enshrined there, then exchange cups of *saké*.

Exchange of Rings

Nowadays even when couples marry at a shrine they often follow the Western custom of exchanging rings.

The Reception

After the short wedding ritual comes the reception, an expensive affair with a long guest list: relatives, friends, superiors from the work place and colleagues, all expecting to be entertained with all kinds of rituals. Receptions are usually held in hotels or special wedding halls which prepare refreshments, a meal, the couple's wardrobe, and presents for the guests (see page 16).

Cake Cutting

Cutting the wedding cake is the first act the bride and groom perform together as a couple. Actually the 'cake' is nothing but a model of an idealized Western-style confection that towers in tiers almost up to the ceiling. Only the area for the knife is a real cake.

The Couple's Entrance

The go-betweens lead the bride and groom into the reception hall, to be greeted by the enthusiastic applause of all present.

The amount depends on the relationship one has with the bride and groom, but is usually from 20,000 to 100,000 yen.

Most guests leave the reception with their presents in a large bag or *furoshiki* (large wrapping cloth).

Giving

It is customary for all invited guests to give money which they have placed in ostentatiously decorated envelopes *shūgi-bukuro*.

Receiving in Return

Guests are of course treated to plenty of alcohol and an elaborate meal. When they leave they are given *hikidé-mono* (presents), cake and other sweet food.

The Honeymoon

The blushing bride and awkward groom might be seen off at the station. Friends and relatives give the traditional *banzai*.

But it is becoming more common for the couple to spend their first night at the hotel where the reception is held. For this reason we now see fewer *banzai*s at stations.

Many honeymoons are spent overseas, with some couples dressing in practically the same style.

Honeymooners are expected to spend part of their time buying souvenirs for friends, relatives, and go-betweens.

Settling Down

Once back in the real world husband and wife will probably settle into a small apartment or condominium, and spend the betrothal money on household items.

In some regions of Japan the bride's parents prepare a dowry. A truck-load of furniture, *kimono* and other items, driven around the neighborhood on its way to delivery, provides a diversion for the curious.

Nowadays some couples invite close relatives and friends to a wedding to be held abroad. This can actually work out cheaper than a reception at an expensive Japanese wedding hall, and can lead to more pleasant memories afterward.

AN ADDITION TO THE FAMILY

出産と育児

Once a child is born the couple becomes a family in every sense of the word. For the wife childbirth is physically and psychologically the most important undertaking of her life. Nowadays a growing number of husbands are doing their part too, assisting in the birth and helping to rear their children.

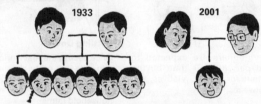

1933   2001

Before World War II it was common for Japanese couples to have five or six children. Times are different now—women marry later, and education is very expensive. These and other factors mean that a woman will bear on the average about 1.4 children in her lifetime. This very low number has serious consequences for future population levels.

Years ago women gave birth in the home, assisted by a mid-wife. Such rudimentary conditions at times resulted in tragedy.

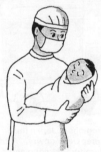

Almost all children today are born in a modern hospital, which also conducts medical examinations before the birth.

Every pregnant woman obtains a "Mother and Child handbook" (*boshitechō*) from her city office. This keeps a record of the pregnancy, birth and the child's development.

It is becoming more common for pregnant women to participate in maternity swimming and/or aerobics after the middle of the second trimester.

Many salaried men would find it hard to get away from work to assist the wife during labor. And with the husband away from home from early morning to quite late at night, in many cases the wife is left on her own to raise the offspring.

The stay in the hospital lasts about one week. After giving birth the new mother spends time recovering and learning the basics: nursing and washing the little one.

Childcare

After leaving hospital it is common for mother and child to spend about a month at the home of the maternal grandparents. This is a good opportunity to learn more about child rearing from the grandmother, and to recover strength.

Since ancient times Japanese babies have always lain on their backs. In the past if the child lay still a lot the back of his head could become flat.

Usually the newcomer sleeps in his parents' room, on the same *futon* as his mother. Japanese houses rarely have space for a baby room, so the married couple must forget the privacy they once had.

During weaning the baby is expected to lap up soft food like *o-kayu* (rice gruel) and noodles, though a growing number of parents now buy Western-style baby food.

Working women, if they are lucky enough to find a nursery, have that option once their maternity leave is over. The scarcity of day nurseries has become a social issue.

As the child grows many parents think he needs brand-name goods and an early start in acquiring skills like swimming and English.

If the young family lives with the husband's parents, trouble can develop between the wife and her mother-in-law, because of differing approaches to child rearing.

On the other hand, a wife in a nuclear family may end up depressed, spending the entire day alone with her young charge.

SCHOOLING

教育

Since World War II Japanese education has followed the American pattern: 6 years elementary, 3 years junior high, and 3 years senior high school. The first 9 years are compulsory. Senior high education is not free. This system gives equal opportunity to all at the lower grades, but has led to tremendous competition to get into the best institutions.

Kindergarten is not compulsory, but most children attend it for one to three years. Here they learn how to adapt to the group, and may acquire simple writing skills. Some kindergartens coach their young pupils in how to enter elite elementary schools.

School starts at the age of 6. Youngsters set off with textbooks, writing materials and who knows what crammed into knapsacks on their backs. These knapsacks are called 'randoseru', from the Dutch word 'ransel.'

School Lunch Program

Elementary schools (and some junior highs) provide lunch for students in their classrooms. Nowadays some schools even have a lunchroom.

Many youngsters have little time for play after school, being busy with other things to learn or *juku* prep school.

Once in a while parents are invited to attend their children's classes. But their presence wakes things somewhat artificial.

The teacher also visits students' homes, to discuss how things are going.

School Trips (*shūgaku-ryokō*)

Schools organize trips to teach students about customs and places different from their own, and to broaden their experience.

At the junior and senior high level, some schools take everyone overseas.

Athletic junior high graduates might be scouted by private senior high schools which will waive entrance requirements and pay their tuition, in exchange for raising the school's sports image.

Some famous institutions offer the entire educational spectrum, from kindergarten to graduate school. It might be difficult to squeeze into kindergarten or primary school, but once you are in it's a smooth ride, with no entrance exams required to move on to a higher level.

But others find competition steep, especially for prestigious national universities and some private institutions. Many a student goes through examination hell.

Those who fail the university entrance exams will most likely spend the following year at a prep school.

Once one qualifies for university, graduation is almost guaranteed. So a good part of a student's energy is spent having a good time or working at a part time job.

Nowadays a number of high school graduates choose to study at a special college in order to master a skill.

Something new in Japan is the idea of education as a lifetime venture. Adults can take advantage of lectures given on television, and some universities now open their doors to older people.

Society is anxious about the negative side of school life too: pupils forever engrossed in comic books, cartoons, and computer games, or worse, needling and bullying, which leads occasionally to suicide or death.

GETTING A JOB

就職

The workplace and society as a whole are becoming more relaxed and flexible, yet the general rule remains the same: men are expected to find a job and keep it until retirement. So graduates search out large, respected companies that offer stable employment with prospects for future advancement.

Fashion for Job Hunters

Hair in place, newly cut.

A dress or feminine suit that presents a trim, neat appearance.

suitable tie

dark suit

A large envelope for the curriculum vitae.

a large envelope

Heels not too high, yet not too low.

black shoes

Graduation is in March. Students hope to enter a company in April. Around April the previous year pressure builds, with young men and women alike knocking on doors, dressed in their best clothes to make a good impression.

University-Company Teamwork
(Shūshoku-kyōtei)

University and company officials often fix the date on which screening and interviews begin. The idea here is to assure fairness. But some students and companies prefer not to respect this arrangement.

Aotagai

Some companies do not wait for applicants to come knocking. They grab the best beforehand. This practice is called *aotagai*, buying up rice before it is harvested.

Some large companies rent large halls, like a martial art gymnasium, for ceremonies that welcome new employees to the fold.

Newcomers are extensively trained before and after entering the company. Training might include rigorous morning to night sessions for several days, with everyone staying together.

THE CHILD STARTS ANOTHER FAMILY

子供の結婚

Parents take the marriage of their children very seriously. Years ago an unmarried woman over 25 would be subjected to a variety of pressures to marry, and relatives and parents would look around for a suitable man. But things are more relaxed now.

Arranged Marriages: The *Miai*

The first major step for an arranged marriage is the *miai*: go-betweens set up a formal meeting between the young man and woman. The aim here, understood by all, is to consider whether the other person would make a suitable life partner. Things naturally tend to get rather formal and tense.

But before the meeting there is an exchange of pictures and curriculum vitae. At this stage it is easy to refuse to go further.

At the *miai* the woman often wears a long-sleeved *kimono*.

Love Marriages

Nowadays more couples marry for love than through arrangement. If the parents object the match may fall apart. Another option is to elope, leaving family relations in temporary chaos.

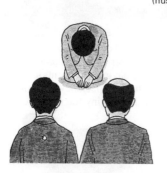

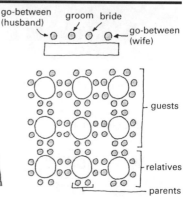

go-between (husband)   groom   bride   go-between (wife)

guests

relatives

parents

On the wedding day it is a custom for the bride to take her parents' hands and thank them for all past favors. This is an emotional moment, the point in time when the daughter finally leaves the nest for a different world.

At the wedding reception parents and other relatives are seated at the back of the room, the furthest away from the bride and groom.

This is the moment for the parents to break down in tears.

¥5,000,000

But parents are not forgotten. One ceremony, conducted at the end of the reception, has the bride and groom present bouquets of flowers to each set of parents, as a form of thanks.

There is another cause for grief: the bill for the wedding and reception. In many cases parents are expected to pick up the tab. It can run from one to five million yen.

'Jukunen', a word that was invented at the end of the 1970s, refers to someone of maturity blessed with ample experience. *Jukunen* are in their 50s and 60s; children have left home, leaving the parents to look inward at their own life and future. With life expectancy now more than 80, the question is how to feel fulfilled during the many years that remain.

Retirement

Most companies have a compulsory retirement policy. For about 70% the age to leave is 60. Yet the possibility of re-employment in the same company, or another, often exists, though in neither case is the salary close to what it was.

Nuré-ochiba-zoku:
Clammy, fallen leaves

The retired husband, not knowing what to do with his freedom, might mope around the house and follow his wife around. He has joined the caste called *'nuré-ochiba'*: in the autumn of life the leaves have fallen *('ochiba')*, to stick clammily *('nuré')* to the wife.

Retirement, Then Divorce

After retirement, the husband's continual presence in the home often makes his wife irritable. A growing number of these women are demanding divorce.

The majority who stick together may nevertheless find their home an empty, gloomy, nest.

But with the arrival of grandchildren things brighten, especially for the grandmother who finds plenty to do.

At New Year's and during the Buddhist festival of *O-Bon* (mid-August) children usually take their offspring to visit their aging parents.

Players use a wooden mallet to hit balls through three gates (arches) in order. The balls must then hit the goalpost.
Teams of five compete against each other.

'Universities' for the Aged

There are other ways to occupy the twilight years, for example university-type courses, even post-graduate lectures, organized by local governments.

Gateball

The European game of croquet has been simplified by the Japanese. Gateball, as it is called, has rapidly spread among the old as an excellent way to keep fit.

Medical costs are negligible for those who have reached the age of 70. Maybe this is why hospital waiting rooms often seem like a hangout for the neighborhood elderly.

More than 50% of Japan's elderly live with a grown child. A common stereotype, unfortunately all too true, is the young wife who must put up with her mother-in-law's nagging.

Other old people, perhaps because they have no children, end up in an old folk's home. Some of these institutions are like elegant hotels, but one must pay for such luxury.

Rent-A-Family

A trend raising eyebrows is a new type of business geared for the lonely: though it costs upwards of 100,000 yen, some childless old folk ask the company to send "children" and "grandchildren" to spend a few hours with them.

CHAPTER 2

EVERYDAY LIFE
家族の生活

Shoes are removed at the entrance. Wearing them in the house is taboo. The idea here is that the floor is to remain clean enough to sit on (even lay down on). Since one's line of vision is low, Japanese ceilings are lower than in other countries. Slippers are sometimes worn in rooms that have no *tatami* (e.g. Western-style rooms, kitchen, corridor).

Apartment Living

Apartment buildings are usually wooden-frame, two-story structures. Rent is relatively cheap. Students and singles gravitate to this form of living.

Monthly rent depends on location, facilities and size, generally ranging from 40,000 to 90,000 yen for one-room with bath, toilet, and kitchen.

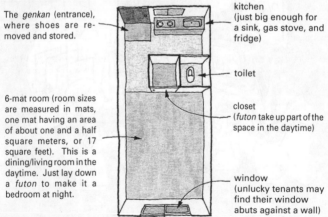

The *genkan* (entrance), where shoes are removed and stored.

kitchen (just big enough for a sink, gas stove, and fridge)

toilet

6-mat room (room sizes are measured in mats, one mat having an area of about one and a half square meters, or 17 square feet). This is a dining/living room in the daytime. Just lay down a *futon* to make it a bedroom at night.

closet (*futon* take up part of the space in the daytime)

window (unlucky tenants may find their window abuts against a wall)

One Step Up

Multiple-dwelling buildings are more solidly built, and for some reason are called *"mansions"* in Japanese. (Sometimes a *"mansion"* is a condominium owned by the occupant.) With the exception of the one-room condo (see page 178), mansions run from a small 2DK to a relatively large 4LDK. (DK = dining/kitchen; LD = living/dining; numerals are the number of other main rooms.)

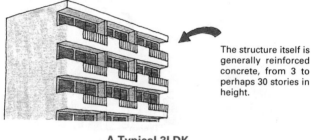

The structure itself is generally reinforced concrete, from 3 to perhaps 30 stories in height.

A Typical 3LDK

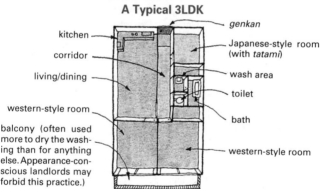

kitchen

corridor

living/dining

western-style room

balcony (often used more to dry the washing than for anything else. Appearance-conscious landlords may forbid this practice.)

genkan

Japanese-style room (with *tatami*)

wash area

toilet

bath

western-style room

Design is a cross between Japanese traditional and Western functional. But dense population has precluded the separate dining room so common in the West. A compromise is the room called "dining/kitchen."

Contractors may liberate the kitchen by constructing a room called "living/dining", but this hardly increases the area.

Single Dwellings

Flat land in Japan is limited. Demand exceeds supply, so urban land prices have sky-rocketed. If you want a house with a small garden you generally have to live far from your company. This means hours on the train every day.

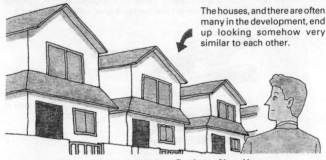

The houses, and there are often many in the development, end up looking somehow very similar to each other.

The traditional Japanese home is a one story structure on a large plot of land. Urban concentration has led to two stories with a pocket garden.

Buying a New Home

Real estate brokers carve out a lot on which they build houses, each one separated by a tiny garden.

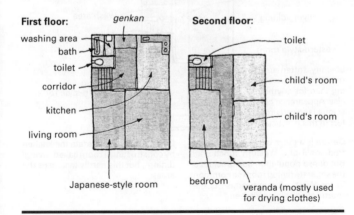

First floor:

genkan
washing area
bath
toilet
corridor
kitchen
living room
Japanese-style room

Second floor:

toilet
child's room
child's room
bedroom
veranda (mostly used for drying clothes)

Two Generations Under One Roof

Since young married couples find it hard to buy their own home, a practical solution is to move in with one set of parents. But this does not mean sharing everything—a new house can be designed so you don't get in each other's hair (and older homes can be remodeled with the same aim in mind).

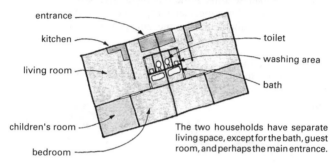

entrance

kitchen

toilet

washing area

living room

bath

children's room

bedroom

The two households have separate living space, except for the bath, guest room, and perhaps the main entrance.

Another Lifestyle:

The Apartment Complex

The apartment complex presents the appearance of row upon row of reinforced concrete high-rises. These are mammoth projects, hardly attractive, but they have the advantage of being near parks, schools and shopping centers. You'll have a long wait (perhaps years) for a parking space, though.

Company-owned Apartments and Dormitories

Large companies build apartment blocks (mostly 2DKs) for some married employees, and dormitories for singles whose homes are far away. Much of the rent is shouldered by the company. This is an advantage, but the disadvantages are obvious to everyone.

When the Japanese think of the "happy family," what often springs to mind is sitting down together at mealtime. Thus the trend toward eating alone— father and kids squeezing in a meal between work or studies—is considered a social problem.

Traditional Japanese Cuisine

When it comes to food Japan is an international society, yet traditional Japanese cuisine certainly holds its own.

Grilling

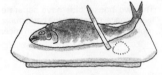

Yaki-zakana: fish barbecued on a wire grill, sprinkled liberally with salt.

Frying

Yasai-itamé: simplicity itself. Sliced cabbage, onion, carrot, bean sprouts and other vegetables fried over a hot fire, with salt and pepper for seasoning.

Deep-frying

Tempura: adapted from Portuguese cuisine centuries ago. A wide variety of vegetables (carrot, lotus root, mushrooms, etc.) and seafood (prawns, squid, fish) are dipped in batter, then deep-fried. (Dip them in a sauce flavored with grated *daikon* radish, and you will praise this Japanese adaptation.)

Croquettes: balls of mashed boiled potato mixed with minced meat and onion, dipped in a thick batter then deep-fried.

Simmering

Ni-zakana: fish simmered in a stock flavored with soy sauce, sugar and *mirin* (sweet *saké*).

O-den: potato, daikon radish, fish cake, boiled egg, etc., simmered until everything takes on the taste of the stock. A bit of mustard goes well with this working-class dish.

Steaming

Chawan-mushi: small pieces of *shiitaké* mushrooms, chicken, fish cake and ginko nuts added to a stock thickened with egg. Steamed in a small earthenware covered pot.

Dressing

Goma-aé: vegetables (such as boiled spinach) in a dressing of sesame paste, sugar and soy sauce.

Pickling

Nuka-zuké: vegetables (such as cucumber and eggplant) pickled in a salty rice-bran paste.

Raw

Sashimi: Thin slices of raw fish or shellfish. Dip in soy sauce made tangy with *wasabi* (horseradish) and you hardly notice the rawness.

A Typical Day's Menu

Traditional Japanese cuisine draws from seasonal ingredients available at that time of the year. But modern influences have brought us instant and fast-food varieties, so the familiar image of Japanese food as low-calorie and healthy is losing out to a reputation of high-salt, high-calorie.
Here is a typical menu for the day, balanced and relatively healthy.

Breakfast

Rice, *miso* soup, fried egg, *nattō* (fermented soybeans), *nori* (dried seaweed), pickles, green tea.
(Nowadays the young crowd shies away from this old-fashioned breakfast, opting for toast, omelet, cereal and coffee.)

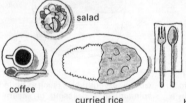

salad

coffee

curried rice

A box lunch brought from home saves time and money.

Lunch

The mid-day meal is usually simple. Those eating out will often choose noodles (*udon* or *soba,* made from wheat and buckwheat respectively). A set lunch with rice and *miso* soup is cheap and nutritious.

Supper

If the father makes it back in time for supper he may have a beer or some *saké* before eating. Western food mixed with Japanese fare seems to suit the kids.

hamburg

pickles

vinegared vegetables

rice

miso soup (*miso-shiru*)

Supper in the Urban Home

Since World War II, eating habits and manners have changed greatly.

Years ago the whole family sat on *tatami* around a low table. This was a time to relax and enjoy each other's company.

Nowadays the television has taken over: it can be a form of relaxation during the meal, but the supper atmosphere is far different from the good old days.

In any case, the father probably works far from home, so comes home much too late to eat with anyone.

The kids may have had a hard day at *juku* (prep school), so often end up eating alone. This is hardly conducive to ensuring a good diet.

Snacks

Children stuff themselves with snacks during the day. Potato chips, popcorn, crackers, and candies all make for a disconcerting amount of salt, sugar and additives.

Snacks and candies

Fast food

Fruit

Western-style desserts

Traditional Japanese snacks, not much seen now:

Fukashi-imo: Steamed sweet potato

Daigaku-imo: Cubes of fried sweet potato, glazed with sugar.

Table Manners

Parents used to be strict about table manners. A shrinking number still are.

Before eating a meal, say *"itadakimasu"* ('I will receive.' This is to thank the cook, those who provided the food, and nature in general). *"Gochisō-sama"* ('Thank you for the delicious meal') is considered polite after eating.

Sit with back straight, facing the table. Hold your chopsticks in your right hand. Use your left hand to bring the small soup bowl to your mouth.

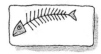

Fish bones are left in a neat, orderly fashion.

The chopsticks on large plates of food in the middle of the table are for bringing the food to your own plate.

Many bowls have covers. Make sure they go back on when you finish eating.

Bad form when using chopsticks:

Holding a bowl and your chopsticks in the same hand.

Pulling a plate towards you with chopsticks.

Spearing food.

HOME SWEET HOME

家族のだんらん

For the dog-tired salaried worker, bliss is simple: relaxing at home on the weekend with wife and kids after the evening meal, chatting or watching TV (probably doing both at the same time). Time together like this is now seen as important in raising well-adjusted children.

A few years ago homes had only one television set.

Disadvantage: fights over which channel to watch; Advantage: more communication.

Affluent living has done away with both of these.

Except for weekends, work and *juku* keep fathers and children away from home until late.

Pets

With fewer children and more money to spend, it is natural that families should adopt an animal as part of the family.

Shetland sheepdog   Pomeranian

Siberian husky   Labrador retriever

American shorthair cat
(popular but expensive)

In the 1950s spitz dogs were quite common as watchdogs, but people were turned off by their shrill barking. Siberian huskies and Labrador retrievers have taken their place.

Less trouble than dogs and cats, and therefore gaining popularity, are exotic reptiles like lizards, snakes and iguanas.

Affluence has spawned a new business, the "pet hotel" for your animal when you are away from home. A dog's "room in the inn" can cost you up to 5,000 yen a day.

Life Day by Day 日常のくらし

JAPANESE TOILETS AND BATHS

トイレと風呂

Toilets and baths are usually in separate closet-size rooms, but apartments, tight for space, may have them both in one unit.

Mastering the Japanese Toilet

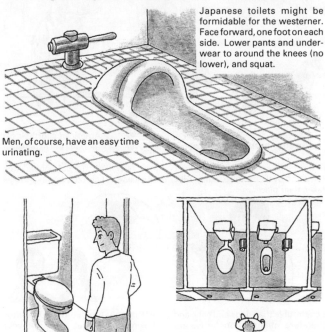

Japanese toilets might be formidable for the westerner. Face forward, one foot on each side. Lower pants and underwear to around the knees (no lower), and squat.

Men, of course, have an easy time urinating.

Western-style toilets are becoming more common in the home, and some public toilets offer you a choice.

Perhaps because it is a land of hot springs, Japan offers a unique form of bathing. The idea is to soak in very hot water up to the neck, letting the day's troubles float away. This is a good chance for Dad to spend time with his small children.

Mastering the Japanese Bath

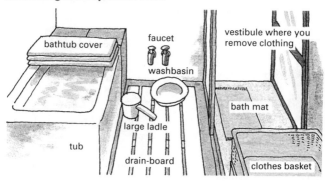

bathtub cover

faucet

washbasin

vestibule where you remove clothing

bath mat

large ladle

tub

drain-board

clothes basket

Remember that the hot water in the tub is to remain clean and soap-free for the next person (and the next and the next). So first wash yourself well on the drainboard (this keeps your feet out of the soapy water), and get rid of all grime and soap first. Only then are you ready to jump into the bath.

A good long soak takes away the stress of the day, but if the water is too hot you might become dizzy.

When you've finished, put back the bathtub cover so that the water remains hot for the next person.

KEEPING THE HOUSE CLEAN
家事のいろいろ

Over the centuries Japanese women have been given the lion's share of housework and rearing children. It is only recently that men do not feel emasculated if they pitch in.

Laundry

washboard

washtub

Japanese washing machines are small but efficient. Clothes are dried on the balcony, facing south if possible.

Years ago water was carried to washtubs. Clothes were scrubbed one by one.

Doing the dishes

Dishwashing machines are rare, and Japanese cuisine calls for an amazing number of small plates, dishes, bowls and covers. Luckily most food is not greasy.

A sign of growing affluence is the dish drier in some homes.

Cleaning

The market offers a vast choice in vacuums, with new functions making the one you own obsolete long before it breaks down.

In the old days a *hataki* knocked dust down to the floor. A *hōki* did the rest.

After *tatami* are vacuumed they are wiped hard with a damp cloth. Wring out the cloth well before using, as *tatami* are made from a plant material that can decay if damp.

Until about 20 years ago autumn leaves on the ground were swept up, then burned with sweet potatoes roasting in the ashes.

Mushiboshi

Japanese summers are very hot and humid. To avoid mold and mildew, clothes (even books) are aired in the sun during the stickiest time of the year.

Year-end *Ō-sōji*

Just before New Year the entire nation goes through a cleaning ritual, getting rid of the year's dirt and grime, especially in areas that have been ignored until then.

SLEEPING

寝る

Some younger people may prefer a bed, but others say they sleep better on a *futon* laid out on the *tatami* floor in the evening.

Japanese bedding

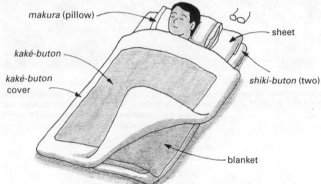

makura (pillow)

sheet

kaké-buton

kaké-buton cover

shiki-buton (two)

blanket

Married couples each have their own set of bedding.
In winter, electric blankets (above or below the body) or electric bed warmers make for a cozy sleep.

Hot water bottles

These are made of metal or ceramic, but are losing out to the convenience of electricity.

**Bedroom at night,
living room during the day**

Japanese *futon* are light and fluffy, easy to fold up and put away in the closet *(oshiiré)* during the day. *Futon* at the bottom, other bedding on the shelf.

Airing *futon*

Futon absorb body moisture. Air them on the balcony on sunny days— they will be fluffier, and nice and warm at night.

How to save space in the closet

Some homes have special plastic bags which compress the *futon*. This is a fad, but it does save space.

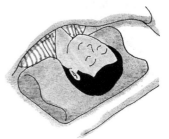

Fad pillows—Do they work?

Japanese consumers go for fads. If you don't sleep well, maybe you need a concave pillow, or a pillow with its own magnetic field, or... Some manufacturers say their pillows get rid of stiff shoulders.

ONE DAY IN THE LIFE OF TWO FAMILIES

家族の一日

Now let's look at two rather typical families, one urban, one rural.

City folk (own a 3LDK condominium—see page 35)

Yamamoto Saburō, 42, climbing up the professional ladder at a large trading firm.

Miyoko, 40, his wife, works part-time at a department store.

Yōsuké, 10, their son, 4th grade.

Miyuki, 3, their daughter.

● ●

Country folk (have owned farmland for generations, live in a large house)

Ishii Yūzō, 41, farmer.

Yoshié, 40, his wife.

Midori, 12, their daughter, 6th grade.

Makoto, 8, their son, 2nd grade.

Keiko, 5 months old, their baby girl.

Yoshio, 65, Yūzō's father.

Kiku, 63, Yūzō's mother.

Kenji, 35, Yūzō's brother, still a bachelor.

5:00 am
Everyone still fast asleep.

6:00 am
Miyoko is making breakfast and box lunches.

● ●

5:00 am
The sun rises, and so does our farming family, going out to do chores.

6:00 am
Yoshié and Midori come back to prepare breakfast.

7:00 am
Everyone at the breakfast table.

8:00 am
Saburō squeezed on all sides in morning rush hour. Yōsuké on his way to school.

7:00 am
Everyone at the breakfast table. Yoshié is giving baby formula to Keiko.

8:00 am
Midori and Makoto off to school, one hour away on foot.

9:00 am
Miyoko takes Miyuki to nursery school.

10:00 am
Miyoko arrives at work.

9:00 am
All adults (except Yoshié, who is house-cleaning) doing farm chores.

10:00 am
Tea break

11:00 am
No-one home.

12:00 noon
All four members of the family eat lunch, but separately. Box lunches for the adults. The children are fed at school and nursery school.

11:00 am
Yoshié and Kiku prepare lunch.

12:00 noon
All adults eat together. The school provides lunch for the two kids.

1:00 pm
Saburō is negotiating with a client.
The house is still empty.

2:00 pm
Yōsuké comes back from school,
letting himself in with his own key.

1:00 pm
Everyone was up at the crack of dawn,
so they feel justified taking a nap.

2:00 pm
Makoto comes back from school,
drops his knapsack, runs off to play
with a friend.

3:00 pm
Yōsuké, still alone, eats something (not nutritious, but refreshing for 10-year olds) in front of the TV.

4:00 pm
Yōsuké leaves for *juku* (prep school).

3:00 pm
Everyone takes a break. Midori comes home.

4:00 pm
Yoshié takes her two daughters to buy groceries for supper.

5:00 pm
Miyoko picks up Miyuki at the nursery school, goes shopping, then returns home.

6:00 pm
Miyoko and Miyuki have supper together. Yōsuké grabs a hamburger during a break in his studies at *juku*.

● ● ● ● ● ● ● ● ● ● ● ● ● ● ● ● ● ● ●

5:00 pm
Yoshié, Midori and Kiku prepare supper. The other adults are tidying up around the farm.

6:00 pm
Everyone sits down to the evening meal.

59

7:00 pm
Miyoko and Miyuki take a bath together. Yōsuké is still at *juku*.

8:00 pm
Saburō is working overtime at the office.

7:00 pm
Everyone in front of the TV, except for Yūzō and Kenji, who leave for a local meeting.

8:00 pm
Taking turns having a bath. Kids do their homework.

9:00 pm
Miyuki goes to bed (half willingly). Yōsuké comes back from *juku*, eats supper alone. Miyoko does the ironing.

10:00 pm
Saburō still not home. Miyoko sits up for him, a lonely figure in the night.

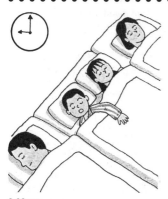

9:00 pm
Yūzō and Kenji return. Everyone goes to bed.

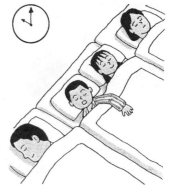

10:00 pm
The house is quiet, except for a few snores.

WHAT DO MEN DO IN THEIR TIME OFF?
父の趣味

Marriage does not change many men—they remain interested in the same things as before, though the coming of children may awaken the fatherly instinct in some. Others may dedicate their whole lives to work. These bores have no interests or hobbies whatsoever.

The amateur landscape gardener

Japanese lots may be small, but that does not stop a dedicated gardener. Western influence has brought plants into the house as well.

The amateur musician

School band friendships can be continued by forming an amateur band with one's old classmates.

The budding computer whiz

Some men get a kick out of computer graphics or communicating over telephone lines with their personal computers.

The amateur sportsman

Golfing, skiing, tennis, and of course baseball; these and other sports keep a man fit, both mentally and physically.

Sports does not necessarily mean you have to be fit—you can always watch a game on TV with a beer.

Yet fitness and the environment are "in" now. A fair number of middle-aged people go on day treks in the mountains on weekends.

Gambling

Wives control the purse strings. For some men, gambling (especially at the horse races) is a chance to get rich quick with the pittance their wives give them.

You don't even have to go to the races—bookies will sell you tickets elsewhere.

Pachinko

Pachinko is a pinball game set on end. If you get a ball in a hole, plenty will come out.

Experts can win prizes that are exchanged for prizes.

DO WOMEN EVER HAVE TIME OFF?
母の趣味

For the wife, housework is a perpetual undertaking, on top of which there is the family to look after, and paid work outside the home. But when the children are old enough she might find time for personal interests. These tend to be oriented toward the practical and her own personal appearance.

Gastronomy

In addition to experimenting in new recipes, culinary instincts can find expression in cooking classes.

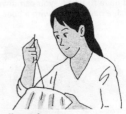

Needlework

Another practical interest is sewing and decorative needlework.

Restaurant hopping

Affluence has led to a new hobby, restaurant hopping. If magazines or TV praise a certain place, women will flock there while hubby and the kids are away during the day.

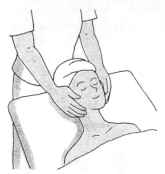

Personal appearance

Beauty salons, aesthetic clinics, aerobic studios, saunas and swimming clubs can make a lot of money off women who want to look young and attractive.

Travel

For some, travel with other women is an opportunity to get away from demanding husband and kids and to feel young and independent again.

Shopping

Hours can be spent browsing through department stores. But time can be saved ordering from catalogues or in television shopping.

Stage managing

Some women's hopes and dreams are projected on their children, who suddenly find themselves in theatrical groups or classes for budding young models and musicians. Mothers' entire lives can be spent dedicated to their children.

CHILDHOOD IS FOR PLAY
子どもの遊び

Japanese childhood games have their origins in the distant past, but of course modern technology and other cultures are important influences too. Unfortunately, today's demands for scholastic achievement have cut down on time spent with friends or just being oneself.

Oni-gokko

What country does not have the game of tag? The first *oni* (devil) is the one who loses *jan-ken*. The person who is tagged becomes the next *oni*.

Kakurembo

Hide-and-seek is universal too. Here again *jan-ken* determines the *oni*. The next *oni* is the first kid found.

Kan-keri

This game is like *kakurembo*, with an added twist: the *oni*'s base is a can on the ground. The *oni* has to find all of the others; in the meantime they try to sneak back and kick his can.

If the can is kicked, everyone already discovered has another chance at hiding.

Ishi-keri

A kind of hopscotch, for girls. Draw squares on the ground. Stand on only one foot. Kick a stone into a square, jumping into it at the same time. Continue like this until the end. You are out if your other foot touches the ground, or if your stone ends up outside the enclosed space.

Nawa-tobi

Skipping, in tune to a song sung by other girls.

Sports

Many boys join a baseball or soccer team. But this is close to boot camp: hours and hours of practice, then matches with other teams.

Computer games

If friends are all busy at *juku* or elsewhere, computer games in front of the TV set can while away the time.

Jan-ken

A good way to pick an instant winner. Hands make the shape of a stone, scissors or paper.

Stone wins over scissors, since it is harder.

Scissors win over paper, obviously.

Paper wins over stone, since it can wrap around the stone.

In a group, everyone chants *"jan-ken-pon"* together, thrusting out their hands at *"pon."*

IS OLD AGE FOR LEISURE?

老後の趣味

Retirement means lots of spare time.

Bonsai

When planted in a ceramic pot, trees can be restricted through repeated cutting and limits on soil and fertilizer. Nature in miniature.

Different *bonsai* styles

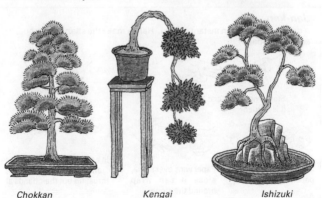

Chokkan   *Kengai*   *Ishizuki*

Use a mallet to hit wooden balls through three hoops, in order, then hit the goal pole.

Gateball

The Japanese version of croquet has gained much popularity among the elderly. Five players on each of two teams.

Theater Going

Older women may have the time and means to dress up and enjoy the theater. Perhaps a *Kabuki* play, fantasies out of the Edo period (1615-1867).

Volunteer work

The community benefits greatly from public-spirited elderly people who cut grass in parks and pick up after boors who litter.

Other enjoyments are *karaoké* parties, sketching, and married couples enjoying, finally, time together on a trip.

FAMILY TOGETHERNESS

家族ですごす

A working man's time off usually consists of three one-week vacations a year. But everyone is on holiday at the same time, so trains, planes and expressways, and the destinations they lead to, are packed.

The first week is New Years. This is a time of celebration, with a visit to a shrine or temple, perhaps in traditional dress.

The second holiday season is "Golden Week," when a number of national holidays come close on the heels of one another at the end of April and beginning of May. Families with children celebrate Children's Day on May 5.

The third week off is in mid-August. *O-Bon* is a Buddhist festival commemorating those in the family who have died. This is the customary time to go back to the ancestral home and visit the cemetery.

Going home

New Years and *O-Bon* are times to visit one's place of birth. But the wife might find her husband's former home constricting, and the husband might be positively bored at his wife's parents' house.

Travel

Hot springs and tourist spots are obvious destinations to get away from it all. But if you are a family of four you could be set back about 100,000 yen a day.

A trip to the zoo

The old-fashioned zoo, with animals cooped up in small cages, is gradually changing to a more open, natural style.

Amusement parks

Roller coasters are a way to test your lungs' screaming capacity. Lines for the best rides can be up to two hours long.

Shopping

A family trip to a department store may be the Japanese mother's ideal outing, but poor old Dad is bound to come back all worn out.

Eating out

"Family restaurants" have ample parking space and food to suit the tastes of each person.

Parks

Practically the cheapest way to spend the day is in the park, playing catch or, say, badminton.

Staying home

What could be cheaper than doing nothing at home? (Here TV and computer games are included as 'nothing.')

CHAPTER
3

FESTIVITIES
THROUGHOUT THE YEAR
家族の四季

NEW YEAR (January 1)
正月 (1月1日)

With the exception of the service industries, the entire country goes on holiday. This is family time, with most working fathers on paid leave from about December 28 to January 5. The New Year is also the time to return to one's roots: Japanese food, games, *kimono*, and prayers at a *Shintō* shrine or Buddhist temple.

O-sechi ryōri

Food for the new year is distinctly traditional, usually served in *jūbako* (tiers of square, lacquered wooden boxes). One fish that will surely be served is *tai* (red snapper, red being the color of good fortune, and *medetai* meaning a joyous occasion). Food for many meals is prepared by December 31, so that housewives, too, can be freed from the kitchen at least during this festive part of the year.

Kagami-mochi

These are a pair of rice cakes, the smaller one placed on top of the larger, decorating a place of honor such as the household altar.

Otoshi-dama

Originally meant as a present to celebrate the New Year, *otoshi-dama* have degenerated into gifts of money for children. Little hands quickly unwrap the paper envelope to answer the question on every curious tongue, "How much?"

At other times of the year, few people wear *kimono* in the home, but the New Year is an exception.

Shimé-nawa

Many homes hang this New Year decoration outside the home (at the entrance or gate) to ward off evil. Shimé-nawa are hung at Shintō shrines throughout the year, to show the boundary between a sacred place and the ordinary world.

Kadomatsu

Kadomatsu are placed outside the entrance, one on each side. The toshigami, a god who brings good harvests and greater profits, dwells inside. This simple New Year decoration is made of bamboo stalks and pine boughs, bound together with straw.

Hanetsuki

This New Year girls' game is rarely played anymore. Those who fail to hit the shuttlecock with their wooden paddle (hagoita) get their faces daubed with India ink.

Money is given to the performers.

Hatsu-mōdé

It is customary to pray for health, wealth and happiness during the coming year. The crush starts on New Year's Eve, with famous shrines and temples packed solid.

Shishi-mai

Another custom, unfortunately seen less frequently than before, is the lion dance. The dancing lion exorcises malignant spirits. Performers pass from house to house to pray for the family's material success.

Local New Year's Celebrations

The entire nation is swept up in the mood of the New Year. Each region has its own traditions for this beginning of a new cycle.

Kemari (January 4, Shimogamo Shrine and other places, Kyoto)

A game popular among 10th century nobles. The idea is to keep a leather ball off the ground by kicking it. The game is re-enacted by players wearing period costumes.

Karuta Hajimé (January 3, Yasaka Shrine, Kyoto)

Another game from the 10th century, also played in the court dress of the time. Cards, spread out before the players, each have the last two lines of a famous *tanka* poem. One person reads the first half, making everyone else scramble for the ending they (hopefully) remember.

Wakakusa-yama Yaki (The second Sunday in Jan., Wakakusa-yama, Nara)

East of the city of Nara is a 342 meter (1,122 ft.) hill, covered with grass. The dead grass is burned off on the day. The flames at night are most impressive, and attract many sightseers. Because the turf is burned, young grass will grow all the stronger in the spring.

Yanaizu Hadaka Mairi (January 7, Yanaizu, Fukushima Prefecture)

Many areas of Japan have *Hadaka Matsuri*, festivals with throngs of men dressed only in loincloths. This one, held at the coldest time of the year, starts with the morning ringing of a temple bell. Young men, practically naked, vie with each other to be the first to climb a thick rope suspended from the temple ceiling. The first one up is assured a year of good luck and happiness.

Sagichō (Mid-January, performed throughout the country)

The community gathers together to burn the New Year decorations (*shimé-nawa, kadomatsu,* etc.). Those who bake *mochi* (rice cakes) in the ashes will supposedly avoid sickness that year.

Tōka Ebisu (January 9 - 11, Imamiya Ebisu Shrine and other places, Osaka)

Ebisu is one of the seven gods of good fortune, venerated as the god of fishermen and merchants. Many people go to buy stalks of bamboo grass, to which charms symbolizing treasure are tied.

The scramble for good luck is good-humored, with loud shouts of, *"Shōbai hanjō dé sasa, motté koi!"* ("Give me some *sasa* leaves to make me rich!")

COMING-OF-AGE CEREMONY (The second Monday in Jan.)
成人式（1月第2月曜日）

This national holiday honors all those who have achieved adulthood (at the age of 20). Local government authorities hold special ceremonies for these young men and women, as well as for their parents, who are so often torn between conflicting emotions.

The long-sleeved *kimono* (*furi-sodé*) costs 300,000 yen and up (way up, even above 1,000,000 yen). For this reason many *furi-sodé* are rented. Still, even a rented one could set you back 200,000 yen.

This is an ideal chance for young adults to dress up, men in suits or *mon-tsuki hakama*, women in long-sleeved *kimono*, the sign of a young un-married woman.

The ceremony itself, held in the city gymnasium or auditorium, is often a bore for the young people—congratulatory speeches of exhortation, given by the mayor or a famous person. Gifts like photo albums are given to the young stars of the day.

Being an adult (20 years or older) means you have the right to vote, smoke and drink alcohol.

SETSUBUN (February 3)
節分 (2月3日)

Setsubun is the eve of the first day of spring. Roasted soybeans are tossed outside the house, with the chant, *"Oni wa soto!"* ("Out with the devil!"). To complement this, other beans are scattered in the house, while chanting *"Fuku wa uchi!"* ("In with good luck!")

roasted soy beans

masu (a square box, formerly used to measure small amounts of liquids or grains)

Often the father wears a devil mask, and is tossed out of the house by the kids throwing beans at him. (Demons are symbols of sickness or natural disaster.)

This event is also held at shrines and temples. Famous *sumō* wrestlers and stars throw beans at the throngs of people gathered there.

Some of the beans are eaten—the same number as your age. This is supposed to ward off sickness during the year.

HINA MATSURI (March 3)
ひなまつり (3月3日)

Hina are dolls representing the Emperor, Empress, and members of the ancient Japanese court. Homes that are blessed with a daughter will display *hina* dolls. The feeling here is to give thanks for the daughter's good health. This is a traditional festivity, but modern girls, too, enjoy taking their treasured dolls out of their boxes one at a time and displaying them on a tiered stand.

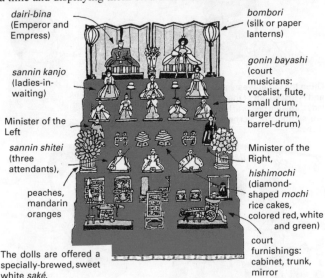

dairi-bina
(Emperor and Empress)

bombori
(silk or paper lanterns)

sannin kanjo
(ladies-in-waiting)

gonin bayashi
(court musicians: vocalist, flute, small drum, larger drum, barrel-drum)

Minister of the Left

sannin shitei
(three attendants),

Minister of the Right,

peaches, mandarin oranges

hishimochi
(diamond-shaped *mochi* rice cakes, colored red, white and green)

The dolls are offered a specially-brewed, sweet white *saké*.

court furnishings: cabinet, trunk, mirror

A set of *hina* dolls can be a simplified version (two or five dolls), or could be so numerous that 11 tiers are needed. Prices vary as well, from 100,000 to 1,000,000 yen. It is often the grandparents who buy a *hina* set after the birth of a granddaughter.

This is the little girl's special day, and a special girl might be given a *hifu* (a small lady's coat) to wear over her *kimono*. Photos are taken to be kept for future years.

The *hina matsuri* would not be complete without a special menu drawing heavily on shellfish, clam soup and shellfish *sushi* being examples.

Variations on the *hina matsuri* tradition

Nagashi-bina

In some areas, dolls are taken to a river or the sea on the evening of March 3, then allowed to drift off and disappear. This ritual placates the spirits of calamity, to ensure no trouble in the coming year.

Kodomo-bina

At Myōen-ji temple in Tokyo, you can see an unusual festival: children themselves dress up as ancient court personages, and arrange themselves on tiers— living *hina* dolls.

RITES OF PASSAGE IN THE EDUCATION SYSTEM

卒業式と入学式 (3月～4月)

Japan's students pass through kindergarten, elementary school, junior high and senior high to arrive at the university level. March is the time for graduation ceremonies, with entrance ceremonies being held in April.

During the graduation ceremony, speeches are given by the principal and special guests, then each graduate is called to the stage to receive a certificate.

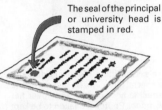

The seal of the principal or university head is stamped in red.

The graduation certificate

The print is in a formal writing style.

Many university students go on a graduation trip (*sotsugyō ryokō*). This is their last chance to enjoy themselves before settling into a job. With the coming of affluence some such trips are often to overseas destinations, and can last a number of weeks.

Graduates of junior and senior high schools, in the throes of adolescence, have their own special rituals. A girl may have her eye on a special boy. If she can get him to give her a button from the jacket of his uniform—specifically the second from the top—chances are her crush is not one-sided.

Entrance ceremonies

These ceremonies are an occasion for mothers to wear something formal, maybe even a *kimono*.

Entrance ceremonies are usually held in the first part of April, at the beginning of the scholastic year. In many parts of Japan this is cherry blossom season: the beginning of spring and a new beginning for youth.

Different university clubs vie with each other, trying to grab new recruits before they are snapped up by another club.

New club members are welcomed with a party. Freshmen are almost all 18 or 19 years old, and so are not legally allowed to drink. But sometimes the seniors get carried away, and some poor freshmen end up in the hospital with a case of acute alcohol poisoning.

CHILDREN'S DAY (May 5) AND GOLDEN WEEK
子どもの日 (5月5日) 〜ゴールデンウィーク〜

March 3 (the third day of the third month) is Girl's Day. Before the war, May 5 was Boy's Day, but now it is a national holiday to honor all children. A family with a boy will display a miniature set of medieval armor in the house, and a set of flying carp (*koinobori*) streamers outside. These objects remind us of the boy's masculine strength and vigor.

Flying carp

If you see these carp banners fluttering above a house, you can assume the family has at least one boy. Shaped and flown like an airport windsock, these cloth fish "swim" into the wind. It is hoped that boys will face the adversities of life in the same way, and thereby achieve success.

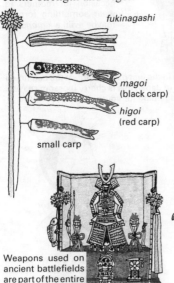

fukinagashi

magoi
(black carp)

higoi
(red carp)

small carp

Gogatsu ningyō

In the hope that the boy will grow up sound in body and spirit, families display a miniature version of the armor and helmet of a *samurai* warrior.

Weapons used on ancient battlefields are part of the entire set.

Some homes are too small to display the full costume, but merchants have an answer to this dilemma: you can buy just the helmet instead.

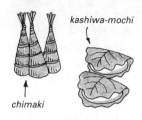

kashiwa-mochi

chimaki

For centuries it has been a custom to eat *chimaki* and *kashiwa-mochi* during the Boy's Festival. *Chimaki* are rice dumplings; because they are rolled in bamboo leaves, they end up conical in shape. *Kashiwa-mochi* are also made with rice flour, stuffed with sweet bean paste and wrapped in an oak (*kashiwa*) leaf.

Another tradition for Boy's Day is to sprinkle the family bath water with the leaves of an evergreen herb, sweet flag. In the old days people would stuff these leaves under the eaves, in the hope of gaining protection from natural calamities.

Injiuchi and shōbukiri

These two games used to be played on Boy's Day. *Injiuchi* was a mock battle: boys would divide into two opposing teams on the beach, then throw pebbles at each other. *Shōbukiri* was played using sweet flag leaves as swords.

Golden Week

Luckily for working people, Boy's Day falls at the end of a string of other national holidays. If the calendar has been kind, a Saturday and Sunday can be added to other days off to make a week—or almost—of paid vacation. It is obvious, then, why the days from April 29 to May 5 are known by this Anglicism, Golden Week. The only problem is that the whole country seems to be intent on enjoying itself away from home, so trains, roads and tourist spots are jammed.

TANABATA (July 7)

七夕 (7月7日)

The gods allow two stars, one feminine (the Weaver Star), the other masculine (the Cowherd Star), to coincide on the Milky Way once a year. On this day the two celestial lovers can enjoy each others' company in the heavens, while the Japanese enjoy a festival down below. Some localities celebrate the Star Festival on the 7th day of the 7th month of the old lunar calendar (August 7).

Bamboo stalks

You can see which homes are observing the festival, because their gardens will be a riot of colored paper tied to long stalks of bamboo grass. On the papers are written short poems (perhaps of love?) or hopes for the future.

Tanzaku

Waka or *haiku* poems are written on long strips of colored paper called *tanzaku*. Years ago, the hope silently expressed was often to achieve better skill in the fine arts of calligraphy or needlework, but today's wishes are generally more mundane.

Tanabata festivals in Hiratsuka and Sendai

The two most famous *Tanabata* festivals are held annually in Sendai, Miyagi Prefecture (around August 7), and in Hiratsuka, Kanagawa Prefecture (around July 7). Huge decorations with colorful streamers are paraded past throngs of onlookers.

Tanabata-okuri

In some regions, children throw the bamboo and decorations into the river or sea the morning after the festival. Everything floats away, and hopefully happiness will come in return.

SUMMER FESTIVALS (July and August)
夏祭り (7月～8月)

Summer is a time when the rice has been planted, but not yet reaped. Some time can be spared for festivities, and the gods should be placated, since crops must be protected from bad weather. Everyone enjoys the portable shrine parades, and the kids have another object in mind, too: they are given a special allowance to spend on food and souvenirs at stalls set up near the local shrine.

Mikoshi

The shrine god is carried through the town in its own portable *mikoshi*, half-shrine, half-palanquin. Often the roof is adorned with the figure of the mythical phoenix.

Kingyo-sukui

In a shallow tank are goldfish. Your job is to fish them out, into a bag of water. Your only implement is a piece of paper supported by a wire hoop, and wet paper is anything but strong...

Many *yatai* (stalls) set up inside the shrine compound make the festivities even more interesting. People crowd around, everyone makes merry, and the *yatai* owners do a roaring business.

Local Summer Festivals

Festivals are held throughout Japan, throughout the year, but summer festivals put on the best show, as they combine the free spirits which summer weather can induce with the boisterousness of the Japanese as a group. Here are a few of the more famous summer festivals.

Yamahoko Junkō

Floats called *yama* or *hoko* can reach the tremendous height of 20 meters (about 65 feet). 32 of these floats parade through the streets of Kyoto.

Gion Matsuri (July 1 - 29, Yasaka Shrine, Kyoto)

This historic festival originated in 9th century Kyoto. It lasts almost a month, but the two big days are *Yoiyama* on July 16, and *Yamahoko Junkō* on July 17.

Kangen-sai (June 17, according to the lunar calendar, Itsukushima Shrine, in Hiroshima Prefecture)

A *mikoshi*, in which a god is resting, is taken on a voyage across the strait. On the deck of the ship is a small orchestra of wind and string instruments. Their ancient music is meant to placate the god.

Hamaori-sai (July 15, Samukawa Shrine, Kanagawa Prefecture)

More than 30 *mikoshi* are carried into the sea. Loud boisterous shouts rise up from the men jostling against each other. Apparently the gods want things this way—the louder the shouts, the more placated they are.

***Nebuta Matsuri* (August 2 - 7, Aomori, Aomori Prefecture)**

This festival is known for its floats which are actually huge paper lanterns on wheels. The lantern framework is made of bamboo or wire. On the paper are drawn colorful, fanciful figures of *samurai*, demons, birds or wild creatures. At night the light shines from behind, almost like an ancient slide show. The Neputa Festival in Hirosaki is also famous.

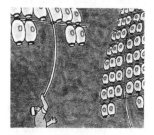

***Kantō* Festival (August 4 - 7, Akita, Akita Prefecture)**

Kantō are long poles of bamboo, about 10 meters (33 ft.) long. From these are attached horizontal bars, used to hang 46 paper lanterns (*chōchin*). You might see 160 *kantō* being paraded around the town.

***Hanagasa Odori* (August 5 - 7, Yamagata, Yamagata Prefecture)**

Thousands of people, with round hats bedecked with artificial flowers, make quite a sight as they dance through the streets of Yamagata. They keep time with shouts of *"Yassho, makasho!"*

THE *BON* FESTIVAL (August 13 - 16)

盆 (8月13〜16日)

According to Buddhist tradition, once a year the souls of people's ancestors make their way back home for a short visit. The spirits are welcomed with special fires and a spirit altar. Each region, indeed each household, has its own way to celebrate the festival—Buddhist sects do not set out rigid rules to follow. In some areas *Bon* is celebrated in July instead of August.

Mukaé-bi

On the night of the 13th, small welcoming fires are lit in front of homes, so that the spirits will not lose their way. Often hemp with the outside covering stripped off is burned.

Shōryōdana

On the morning of the 13th the household Buddhist altar is cleaned. Then a small spirit altar (*shōryōdana*) is set up in front of it.

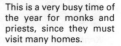

This is a very busy time of the year for monks and priests, since they must visit many homes.

The Buddhist priest reads a sutra at the altar. The souls stay with their families for a few days, arriving on the evening of the 13th, then returning to the spirit world at the end of *Bon* (on the 16th, though in some areas *Bon* ends a day earlier).

Many companies close down at this time of the year, giving employees the chance to return and relax in their hometowns.

On the last day of *Bon*, send-off fires (*okuribi*) are lit in the same places where welcoming fires burned a few days before. In some areas, lanterns and food offered to the souls are taken to a river or the sea, to float off and disappear.

A large circle of people dance around a *yagura* in the center.

On the *yagura* are a large drum and other instruments, which set the beat. Someone well versed in *Bon* dancing will demonstrate the steps (which are simple, actually) on the *yagura*.

Bon dances

Bon dances, songs and music, which have been very popular since the 16th century, welcome the ancestors' spirits back to their native homes.

ATHLETIC MEETS (September or October)
運動会 (9月～10月)

Once the weather cools down a little, people become more sports-minded. All schools, even some companies, organize athletic meets, in which all students (or employees) are expected to participate. Relatives come out in force to watch and lend moral support.

Tama-wari

Two large hollow paper balls are strung up above the ground. The idea is to break these huge balls by throwing small balls at them. The first team to do so wins. When the balls break, pieces of paper come pouring out in a gorgeous fountain of color.

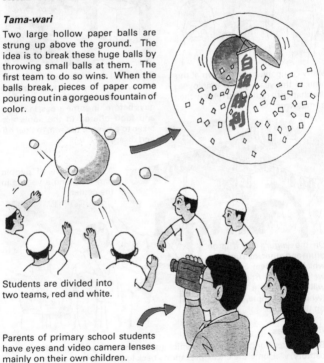

Students are divided into two teams, red and white.

Parents of primary school students have eyes and video camera lenses mainly on their own children.

Some of the competitions

Races

Young kids in the first two years of school run only about 50 meters. A prize is given to the winner.

Kibasen

This is a cavalry battle, each horse being three or four students standing together, with a knight astride each horse. The object is to steal as many caps as possible from the opposing team.

At lunch time the grounds become quiet, for contestants and spectators are eating box lunches.

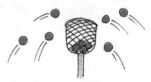

Tama-iré

Two large baskets are set at the top of poles. Red and white compete with each other to see which team can throw the most balls into the baskets.

Tsuna-hiki

The ancient game of tug-of-war.

Cheerleaders do their bit at senior high school and company athletic meets alike.

HARVEST MOON VIEWING (September full moon)
お月見 (9月中旬)

The full moon around the middle of September is the most beautiful of all. Moon gazing is often enjoyed by the entire family, or perhaps by young couples who are stumbling towards a mutual declaration of love. During this time, a room might be decorated with *susuki* pampas grass, which has grown tall by this time of year, and with round cakes.

tsukimi dango
(steamed or boiled dumplings made of flour)

aki no nanakusa
(seven traditional plants of autumn)

autumn fruit

susuki

Some people find a cup (or two) of *saké* make the occasion more memorable.

Kangetsu-é

Parties may be organized beside a pond or in the country, both ideal places for viewing the moon. The *Kangetsu-é* moon viewing party at Daitoku-ji temple in Kyoto is particularly famous. Here you can gaze at the harvest moon from a boat floating in the temple's large pond. The boat is decorated with a dragon's head for added enjoyment.

SHICHI-GO-SAN FESTIVAL (November 15)
七五三 (11月15日)

It is thought that young children should be taken to the parish shrine to ensure a future free of sickness and misfortune. On November 15, three- and five-year-old boys, and three- and seven-year-old girls are presented to the *uji-gami* (local deity).

Shichi-go-san (7-5-3) are numbers associated with luck and festivity (as indeed are other odd numbers, 1 and 9).

Children are dressed in their best clothes, with the girls in *furi-sodé kimono* or fancy dresses.

Chitosé-amé

Chitosé-amé literally means "thousand-year candy," 1000 in this case signifying many, many years of life. The candy itself is a long 30 cm (1 foot) stick, colored red and white. The paper bag is decorated with symbols of luck, such as the pine, bamboo, and plum (commonly grouped together), and the crane and tortoise (sometimes paired).

Newborn infants are also taken to the local shrine, in accordance with the custom, *o-miya-mairi*.

CHRISTMAS EVE AND CHRISTMAS DAY
クリスマス (12月24, 25日)

Less than one percent of Japan's total population is Christian. In any case, the Japanese are by nature more agnostic than religious. Christmas, though, is an excellent chance to enjoy oneself, and provides shopkeepers with great mercantile opportunities.

The Christmas tree

Many families put up a Christmas tree, or rather a plastic imitation of one, which has been stored away for the last year.

But decorations are confined to indoors.

First there is Christmas Eve, celebrated by the whole family—if Dad can make it home—around a table attractively laden with good food.

"Santa Claus" parents put presents near their children's heads while they sleep.

Christmas is not a national holiday, but office parties are common this time of year. Dad may arrive home late, with a face as red as Santa Claus's.

YEAR'S END
年末 (12月下旬)

After the excitement and buoyant feelings of Christmas, the entire nation gets down to the serious business of preparing for the New Year. Winter holidays begin around this time, so the children get into the act too, cleaning the house from second floor ceiling to ground level (Japanese houses have no basements).

One of the biggest jobs is washing windows and scrubbing the accumulation of grease from around the kitchen stove.

This is the time to attack all of the nooks and crannies that have been ignored during the year, a task which calls for muscle, so the father is indispensable at this time.

Another important task is writing New Year messages to be mailed to friends and colleagues. Some people send 30 or so, some send more than a hundred. The post office guarantees delivery on the morning of New Year's Day if you post them by the middle of December.

Mochi-tsuki

An old custom, now unfortunately rarely seen in ordinary homes, is pounding rice to make rice cakes (*mochi*). A highly glutinous variety of rice is steamed, placed in a large wooden mortar (*usu*), then pounded with a heavy wooden mallet (*kiné*).

Ōmisoka

Ōmisoka, New Year's Eve, is a time for the whole family to sit down to a very simple meal of buckwheat noodles (*toshikoshi-soba*). Simple, because the ideal is (or used to be) to live simply. Noodles, because they are long, like one's own life will hopefully be.

Chūgen and *Seibo*

Twice a year one is expected to send gifts to social superiors and to people from whom one has obtained favors. The first time is in the middle of July. These summer gifts are called *chūgen*. Years ago the custom of giving *chūgen* was to celebrate one's having avoided any calamity during the past half year. They were also given in honor of deceased members of the family. At the end of the year one gives *seibo*, which express the same intent as *chūgen*. (The literal meaning of the word *seibo* is "year's end.") Department stores are very busy at these two times of the year.

The value of the gift is one important consideration, so department stores make deciding easier by arranging some items according to price.

One recent variant on this custom is to have the present, such as fresh seafood or fruit, sent directly from the source.

When you buy gifts at a department store, you can ask the clerk to send them for you. This is easier, though somewhat impersonal.

98

Old-fashioned people would say that, since *chūgen* and *seibo* are meant as thanks to those who have been helpful, it is much more polite to take the gift personally.

Those on the receiving end will send a letter or postcard, expressing thanks. But here, too, the modern fixation with convenience has led to thanks by telephone, or—certainly a no-no in some circles—no word of thanks at all.

Gift-giving on other occasions

Chūgen and *seibo* are sent at two fixed times of the year, but other gifts are given when occasion warrants. Examples here are a wedding, the birth of a child, or when someone is sick. Money and other useful things are acceptable at such times.

O-kaeshi

If you want to understand Japanese society, you must learn to appreciate the custom of *o-kaeshi*, giving something in return. When you receive something you could very well be expected to return the favor (though not immediately). The value of this *o-kaeshi* is generally about half of what was received.

BIRTHDAYS

誕生日

The birthdays of adults are not celebrated as they are in the West, but children's birthdays are another rite of passage.

As in many other countries, birthday cakes go over well with the kids.

Then there are birthday parties, which are almost always a great success. The down side here is that some little ones may brood if they are not invited back.

Kanreki

The traditional way of counting days, months and years used a combination of ten calendar signs (*jikkan*) and twelve signs of the zodiac (*jūnishi*). The two sets were used together in combinations to make a cycle of 60 units. When the cycle was complete, one started again. Even today, when someone reaches the age of 60, he is said to start life, or be born, again. "*Kanreki*" is a celebration of the cycle's completion, and the expression of hope for a long life to come.

FATHER'S DAY, MOTHER'S DAY
父の日と母の日

American culture has influenced Japan in many ways. Father's Day (third Sunday in June) and Mother's Day (second Sunday in May) are examples, as is the fact that the mother is somehow more readily remembered than her spouse.

Flower shop owners make sure the carnations catch the eye easily, but capitalistic laws of supply and demand make it almost impossible for children to stretch their allowance and bring home some carnations for Mom.

The traditional gift for mothers is a bouquet of red carnations, but some women are gratified to receive something handmade, or a helping hand around the house.

Flowers or something else Dad will hopefully like are given on Father's Day.

Both days have been commercialized. Persistent advertising campaigns begin about a month before the actual day.

WEDDING ANNIVERSARIES

結婚記念日

Before the war, most marriages were arranged, and Western influence was not as prevalent. But now it is becoming more common to celebrate wedding anniversaries.

The ideal for some couples is to have dinner for two at a restaurant, leaving the kids at home. But the husband's work is likely to tie him up until late, often meaning no celebration at all.

Romantic couples may give each other gifts, with the wife being surprised with a ring or jewelry.

25th and 50th wedding anniversaries are occasions to be celebrated by the entire family.

ANNIVERSARIES OF A RELATIVE'S DEATH
命日

It is common to remember a loved one by observing anniversaries of the death. On such anniversaries (*meinichi*) it is common to place at the household altar something that the deceased liked very much, and to go and pray at the cemetery.

Meinichi are often observed each month on the same date. The first, second and sixth anniversaries are of particular importance. (See page 110 for a description of *hōyō*.) But other anniversaries are also remembered by friends and relatives.

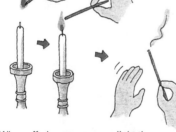

The altar is decorated with flowers and things the deceased was especially fond of.

When offering up a prayer, light the candle, then use its flame to light an incense stick. The stick will start to burn, but do not blow out its flame with your breath—rather, put it out with a small gust of air made by fanning your hand back and forth. Then put the smoking incense stick in the incense stand.

Ring the small gong, then put your palms together in prayer. At a *Shintō* shrine one claps one's hands when one prays, but the Buddhist ritual is more subdued.

WEDDINGS

結婚式のいろいろ

It must be said that most Japanese are not religious, though almost without exception wedding ceremonies are conducted in accordance with the ancient traditions of *Shintō*, Christianity or, in rare cases, Buddhism. *Shintō* weddings are the most common. Previously conducted at one's family's shrine, today most marriages are performed in a shrine built in a modern hotel.

A *Shintō* Wedding

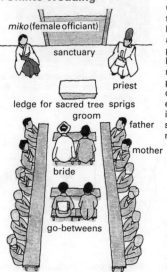

miko (female officiant)

sanctuary

priest

ledge for sacred tree sprigs

groom

father

mother

bride

go-betweens

Bride's immediate family

Groom's immediate family

Generally, only the bride and groom, their immediate families, and the go-betweens attend the religious part of a *Shintō* wedding. After the priest's prayers to the deities (in classical language), the groom makes his marriage oath. Next, the couple performs the *sansan-kudo* exchange of nuptial cups (see page 15), then exchanges rings (a relatively recent innovation). The entire ceremony is surprisingly short, perhaps 20 minutes.

The bride, groom and go-betweens offer sprigs of the sacred *sakaki* tree to the deities.

A Buddhist Wedding

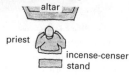

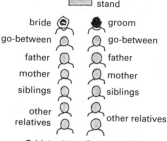

altar

priest

incense-censer
stand

bride   groom

go-between   go-between

father   father

mother   mother

siblings   siblings

other
relatives   other relatives

Bride's side   Groom's side

Japan is, in a sense, a Buddhist country, but the religion is associated more with funerals than with weddings. Buddhist weddings are performed in large temples, with the highest-ranking priest officiating. The priest reports the couple's intentions to the altar, and there is an exchange of rings (as in the Christian tradition) and *saké* cups (as in the *Shintō* ceremony). One difference from other ceremonies, though, is the offering of incense.

All those attending have Buddhist rosaries. (*juzu*).

A Christian Wedding

Less than 1% of Japan's population is Christian, but many young couples think a Christian church wedding is "in." One advantage is that friends can also be present at the actual wedding, unlike in the *Shintō* ceremony.

Sometimes the couple will be asked to attend religion classes some time before the wedding.

FUNERALS
葬式

Daily life in Japan has little connection with religion, but funerals are ceremonies of deep religious significance. The vast majority of funerals are Buddhist. Sutras are read by the priest, and the chief mourner (a family member, perhaps the spouse or elder brother) and the funeral council spokesman (a close friend or relative) have their own roles to play. But behind the scenes, making things run smoothly, is the undertaker. When possible, the body is brought home and given a religious ceremony there, but a temple or hall is used if the house is too small.

A Buddhist funeral

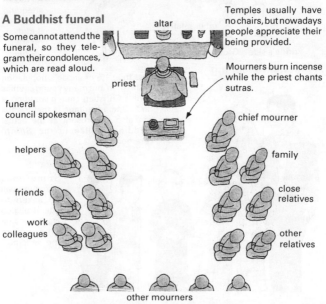

Some cannot attend the funeral, so they telegram their condolences, which are read aloud.

altar

priest

Temples usually have no chairs, but nowadays people appreciate their being provided.

Mourners burn incense while the priest chants sutras.

funeral council spokesman

helpers

friends

work colleagues

chief mourner

family

close relatives

other relatives

other mourners

Preparing the body

The body is washed with hot water and alcohol. The hair is arranged and the face made up a little.

Usually the body is dressed in white clothes (the traveling outfit for the road to Heaven), then placed in a simple coffin.

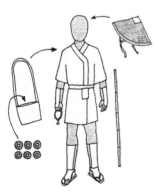

Two chopsticks stand straight up in a bowl heaped with rice (never put your chopsticks like this usually), and a sword is placed close to the head, to ward off evil. The body is always laid with the head towards the north.

The wake

A wake is held the night before the funeral. This is the time for family members, relatives, and friends to gather at the departed person's home. Food and alcohol are served.

Ceremonies in the home

The coffin holding the body is placed under the altar.
(1) Photograph of the deceased
(2) Memorial tablet
(3) Offerings
(4) Flowers (with the name of the person sending them)
(5) Votive lights
(6) Incense censer
(7) Lantern

(1) Take a pinch of incense in your right hand.

(2) Raise it level to your forehead.

(3) Drop it in the incense censer.

(4) Place your hands together in prayer.

Sutras

A priest comes from a temple to read sutras before the home altar.

Those who pay their respects bring *kōden* (literally, "incense money"), which they place on the altar. The envelopes hold from 2000 to 5000 yen, but close relatives give more.

The strings fastening the envelope are tied to make a knot opposite to that used on festive occasions.

Incense

Incense is offered as a prayer for the repose of the soul.
The following is the order followed by some Buddhist sects:

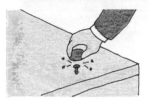

Leaving home for good

The actual climax of the funeral comes when the coffin is carried out of the home, never to return. But first, mourners take turns in an unusual ritual, in which they go through the motions of securing the coffin lid shut with a stone and nail.

The hearse

The coffin is placed in a hearse and taken to the crematorium.

Cremation

The vast majority of bodies are cremated in Japan. The coffin, too, is burned.

Kotsuagé

After cremation, two of the mourners use long chopsticks to pick up certain bones and place them in an urn.

Before entering their own homes, mourners purify themselves with salt.

Final rest

The urn is kept at home for 49 days, then taken to the cemetery for the final rest.

After the funeral, relatives and friends come together for periodic memorial services for the departed.

Sotoba

During each anniversary, a long wooden tablet (*sotoba*) with a sutra written on it is set up behind the tombstone.

Buddhist tradition has established a ritual series of memorial services. As mentioned, the urn is kept in the home for 49 days. Every seven days during this period rites are held at the household altar. Other services are held 100 days after the death, then on anniversaries (*hōyō*) afterward: the 1st, 2nd, 6th, 12th and 16th anniversaries, and even after that.

The memorial service is naturally quite formal: the priest chants sutras, participants burn incense, then they all visit the tomb. In urban areas, with dense populations, cemeteries are often quite far away. You may see a priest on a train traveling to a distant cemetery for the *hōyō*.

The *hōyō* ends with a get-together. Perhaps these gatherings have a formal purpose, but with alcohol flowing and the natural good spirits of the Japanese, the dinner can turn into a party where a good time is had by all.

Higan

Higan is a seven-day Buddhist ceremony to honor the dead, during the spring and fall equinoxes. *Higan*, literally "the other shore," refers to the world of eternal stability awaiting us on the other bank of the river dividing the living from the dead.

Tombs are visited during this time too.

At the beginning of the *Higan* festival, the household Buddhist altar is cleaned and graced with flowers. Food, such as *o-hagi* (rice cake covered with sweet bean paste), and things the departed liked (perhaps *saké* or fruit) is placed at the altar also.

The tombstone is ritually cleansed by pouring a little water over it. Flowers are placed at the base, and incense is burned.

Urns of those placed in the family tomb:	Urns of those not placed in the family tomb:
father mother unmarried children the child who carries on as head of the family, his spouse, their child who carries on as head of the family, etc.	Those who form their own families (i.e., other married children, their spouses, etc.) will establish their own family tombs.

The tomb

Most Japanese have a family tomb behind their own temple, where for generations the family's funerals and memorial services have been held. The grave, then, is a link with one's distant past, and so has much significance in the Japanese psyche.

BUDDHISM AND THE JAPANESE
仏教と日本人

For the average Japanese, the question, "What is your religion?" would be difficult to answer. Almost all families consider themselves members of one of the many Buddhist sects, yet you will find some homes with *Shintō* shrines, and homes where Christmas is celebrated. And there are people who give no thought to religion at all. But one can at least say that the commonly-celebrated Bon festivities (see page 90) and funerals have strong Buddhist overtones.

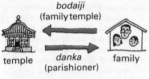

bodaiji
(family temple)

temple

danka
(parishioner)

family

The relationship between temple and household

Family members who are parishioners of a certain temple are called *danka*. They call their temple their *bodaiji*.

Negation of self changed to self-interest

In the idealized form of Buddhism, believers set their sights on achieving happiness in the next world. But somehow Japanese Buddhists have turned that philosophy around, praying instead for what they want in the near future.

Heaven and hell (*gokuraku* and *jigoku*)

For many Buddhist sects, one's life on earth determines whether one will go to heaven or hell. This belief undoubtedly guided people's actions in the past.

The household altar

The traditional Japanese home has a Buddhist altar to show devotion to those who have already passed on. But it may be absent from modern-day households.

En

Many Japanese, even those who are not religious, often refer to *"en." En* is karma, destiny, the idea that certain things happen because they are bound to. This concept comes from Buddhism, and is used to explain good luck (like two people meeting and finding happiness in marriage).

Superstition

Who does not believe certain things happen because of luck, good or bad? Many Japanese people shy away from what they think could jinx them. Some Buddhists have fostered superstitions that insist on a relationship between objects and luck.

Things that bring good luck: Things that bring bad luck:

Having a dream of Mount Fuji, a falcon, or an eggplant during the night after New Year's Day.

A sprig of a tea plant standing vertical in one's teacup.

A crane.

A thong of a *geta* (wooden clog) that breaks.

Cutting one's nails after dark.

A crow.

SHINTŌ AND THE JAPANESE

神道と日本人

Shintō is Japan's indigenous religion, and was well established before the introduction of Buddhism in the 6th century. The practice of *Shintō* is basically limited to specific locations and times. Many activities are associated with *Shintō*, but they are often performed for form's sake, rather than because of a strong feeling of piety.

The mantle for the household gods

Look up near the ceiling in a traditional home, and you may find a small shelf (*kami-dana*) with a miniature shrine for the family gods. On the *kami-dana* you will probably see *saké*, food, or rice. The home could have a Buddhist altar as well.

Going to a shrine

Shrines are very crowded at New Year's, when the whole nation seems to be praying for a successful year. People will go to pray at other times as well, when they need something.

Ema

One common practice is to write one's wish on a wooden tablet (called *ema*), then hang it up within the shrine precincts.

O-mamori

The shrine gives (or rather sells) good-luck charms, *o-mamori*, to be worn to bring good luck and ward off evil.

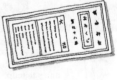

O-mikuji

The shrine will also sell you an *o-mikuji*, a written oracle that tells your fortune. After reading it, people feel either relief or worry.

Salt as purifier

Scientists will tell you salt kills many bacteria—since ancient times the Japanese have used it as a ritual purifier. Some traditionally-minded owners of restaurants, prompted by *Shintō* belief, may place a small mound of salt at the entrance.

Sumō wrestlers throw salt into the ring before their match, to purify the earth.

Ground-breaking ceremonies

Construction means massive changes to the land, so the god living there must be appeased. This is why a *Shintō* ground-breaking ceremony is held.

The mark of the *Shintō torii* (gate)

The *torii* signifies that the land within is sacred.

One might occasionally see a *torii* mark on a garden wall, but this sign only borrows the idea of "purity" to tell all men who feel the urge to relieve themselves that they are in the wrong place.

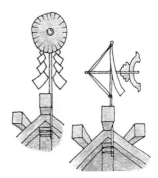

The house is decorated in this way.

Once the building's framework is in place, another *Shintō* ritual is thought advisable.

OTHER BELIEFS
民間信仰

Not all acts of piety or superstitious feelings can be associated with either Buddhist or *Shintō* thought.

Jizō

Jizō are stone images placed along pathways. They look like little monks, and indeed, their origin was influenced by Buddhism. But they belong more to folk beliefs.

Mountains as gods

Mount Fuji receives the most reverence, but other mountains are also considered in a mystic sense. Some people climbing them do so out of devotion.

Dōsojin

These are travelers' guardian deities, set up at village boundaries to protect the village from epidemics or evil spirits. *Dōsojin* also symbolize the village's desire for the prosperity of descendants. In many cases these stone statues represent a pair of deities, one male, the other female.

Devotion to the company

Japanese employees are expected to devote their lives to their companies, to the extent that one could say they have, for all intents and purposes, "caught" religion.

CHAPTER
4

TRADITIONAL AND MODERN CULTURE
外国の人を招く

A VISIT TO A JAPANESE HOME

日本家庭を訪問する

Most Japanese people enjoy having friends visit them. (A word to the wise: you might hear, "Please come and visit us some time," but this might be social posturing.) If you are sure the invitation is sincere, by all means go.

Modern homes usually have a bell, and of course you can knock. But actually the *genkan* (the small entrance vestibule) is considered, in a sense, to be not precisely inside the house—after all, you are still wearing shoes. If there is no answer, you could open the door and call out, *"Konnichi-wa!"* or *"Gomen kudasai!"*

It is slightly bad form to arrive without a gift. Something from your own country is ideal, but fruit, cakes, or the like are fine too. No need to go to great expense.

After the greetings in the *genkan*, you will be invited to "come up" (i.e. take off your shoes and enter). Step up, then point the toes of your shoes toward the door. (Do not turn your back on your hostess—let's call her Mrs. Hashimoto—when removing footwear.)

Mrs. Hashimoto might offer you slippers. (Make sure you don't walk on *tatami* with them; and in the toilet, use the toilet slippers).

(The following scenario is for a formal visit.)

In the *seiza* position, one big toe crosses over the other. Try to look comfortable.

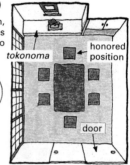

tokonoma — honored position

door

Once in the living room, sit where Mrs. Hashimoto suggests you do. *Tatami* rooms will have cushions (*zabuton*), but don't use one until she insists. Assume the *seiza* position.

In a traditional room, seating arrangements have a pecking order. Generally speaking, the further from the door, or the nearer the *tokonoma* (see page 130), the more honorable the guest.

Probably the only part of the house you will see is the room you are in, the toilet, and the corridor between the two. Other areas are private.

Slide the present forward a little on the *tatami*.

When someone you wish to show respect to is introduced to you, slide off your *zabuton* and resume the *seiza* position.
When you give your present to the host or hostess, say, *"Tsumaranai mono desu ga..."* ('This present is of little interest, but...' This is standard polite form, and is not taken to mean that you are cheap or have poor taste.)

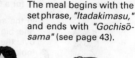

The meal begins with the set phrase, "*Itadakimasu,*" and ends with "*Gochisō-sama*" (see page 43).

Tea will soon arrive. Say "*Itadakimasu*" and draw the cup toward you. If the cup has a cover, put it on the table, top down.

Time your visit so it does not interfere with a meal. But if Mrs. Hashimoto asks you to remain for supper she is probably being sincere. This is a good opportunity to relax more with a Japanese family. They will be happy to tell you about the different ingredients, and how to cook them.

To eat and run is impolite, but so is overstaying your welcome. At the right moment, say "*Soro-soro shitsurei shimasu,*" and assume that any attempt on their part to make you stay longer is pure form.

When your shoes are back on, thanks are due once more for the hospitality. "*Taihen tanoshikatta desu*" ('I had a great time') rounds everything off nicely.

Reading the Japanese Mind

Japanese are said to be reticent in showing emotion. The embarrassed laugh, the vague response, the blank look... These stereotypes are sometimes seen, it is true. But they spring from a fear of causing, or incurring, trouble. Look deeper. Instead of inscrutability, you will find the full gamut of human emotion.

Joy

Don't expect people to jump up and down in excitement, or to dance with joy (except for young sportsmen when they score a point). But even the most reserved old codger will show mirth—just look at his eyes and mouth.

Grief

Bitter tears or wails of grief are rarely seen. The ideal is to endure things stoically. But the lips give things away: they will be tense and sadly pursed.

Anger

It is inadvisable (and perhaps self-defeating) to show bad temper. Any anger felt toward bosses or colleagues is kept in, then vented harmlessly among friends over a glass (or several glasses) of alcohol.

Love

Young people rarely kiss in front of others. Yet they have a way of showing affection that would have raised eyebrows before. Those in their 50s or older will probably never show love in public.

EATING OUT

外食する

It is common for the whole family to eat out together once or twice a month.

Sushi

Except for very young children, the whole family loves *sushi*. The best place to sit is at the counter, where you can watch the server's fancy hand work, an art in itself.

agari
(the word for green tea in a *sushi* shop)

gari
(sliced sweet-pickled ginger)

The *sushi* is placed right in front of you. Take it with chopsticks or in your hand, then dip the *neta* (the top part) in soy sauce.

Count the number of empty plates in front of you, multiply by the unit price, and that's the cost of the meal.

The *sushi* carousel

In some trendy spots, plates of *sushi* go past you on a kind of conveyor belt, like a luggage carousel at an airport. Choose the plates you want. Cheaper than a regular *sushi* bar, so a good bet if you are bringing the kids.

Yaki-niku

Grill the meat at your table, dip it in a sauce, and calculate the cholesterol. Japan has many *yaki-niku* places, each one vying against others for that extra-delicious sauce. (The common elements found in the sauce are soy sauce, *miso* bean paste, garlic, and red pepper.) *Yaki-niku* originated in Korea. All of the words for the side dishes described below are Japanese variants of Korean.

Kimuchi: very spicy, being a pickled mass of salty Chinese cabbage, seafood, *daikon* radish, garlic, red pepper, ginger...

Namuru: Bean sprouts and other vegetables in a dressing of vinegar and red peppers.

Bibimba: Vegetables (in a dressing) and fried egg laid on rice. Mix it all up and dig in.

Kuppa: A hodgepodge soup of rice, *wakamé* seaweed, egg and vegetables.

Some shops give you chewing gum on your way out, because they know your breath might need it.

123

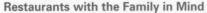

Restaurants with the Family in Mind

These restaurants, usually giant chains, are geared to the car-oriented family living in the suburbs. The exteriors and interiors somehow all look alike (even though this kind of restaurant is found all over Japan).

You and your family can be sure of receiving service with a smile, maybe even a waitress at the door waiting to welcome you with an *"Irasshaimasé!"*

If the restaurant is into new-fangled technology, your order will go via a computerized POS system straight to the kitchen.

The menu has a choice wide enough to suit everyone, young or old alike.

Stuffed toys, candies, and other things likely to please kids are lying in wait near the cash register.

Okonomi-yaki

This Japanese-type pancake is associated with a pleasant, working-class atmosphere. Cabbage, shrimp, squid, and maybe meat are mixed in a batter, then fried on a griddle right in front of you.

(1) Get the iron griddle good and hot, then oil it.

(2) Mix up all the ingredients, then pour them on the griddle, making a round pan-cake form.

(3) 2 or 3 minutes later, turn the okonomi-yaki over (yaki means 'fried').

Don't forget a liberal helping of the sweet sauce and green nori seaweed.

Rāmen

Rāmen, originally a Chinese dish, is now part of Japanese culinary culture. Men means noodle; these firm yellow noodles are made from wheat and egg.

Other food in a rāmen shop has its origins in China too:

In a rāmen shop don't be shy to slurp —rāmen is not for the hoity-toity.

Gyōza: fried dumpling of minced meat and vegetables wrapped in a crescent-shaped wheat shell.

Chāhan: boiled rice and finely-sliced vegetables and meat, mixed together and fried.

電車・バス・タクシー

Trains

Many families now own cars. But when they try to use them for trips, they may wish they had gone by railway, which is fast and efficiently run. Train fares are half-price for primary school students (6 to 12).

Most stations have a ticket-vending machine. Fares (marked on a map above the machine) depend on destination.

Wickets are often automatic in large cities. Put your ticket in the slot: if you didn't pay the correct fare, the gate will close and a buzzer will let you know.

You will want to avoid the weekday rush hour, from 7 to 9 am and from 5 to 7 pm.

But you can always squeeze on; attendants are on the platform to give you a push.

Buses

Japanese buses are an electronic marvel of recorded announcements, lights, buttons, and change machines. City buses may have a uniform fare, or they may follow a rather complicated system, based on distance. In the latter case, take a numbered coupon when you board, then present it to the driver upon disembarking. The number will show where you got on.

Bus stops have a timetable, sometimes even a route map.

Taxis

Taxi fares are almost equally expensive throughout the country, and are based only on time and distance, not number of people or suitcases. The meter is probably equipped to print out a receipt for you.

You can get a taxi at a taxi stand, by telephoning, or by hailing one on the street. Cabs cruising for passengers have a red flag in the window: [空車]

Other useful info: The driver will use a lever at his seat to open and close the back door (on the left side only) for you, so don't touch it—stand out of the way. Don't expect help with your baggage. Tipping is unheard of.

If you get friendly with a family, they might suggest a trip somewhere together. Why not try a hot spring, and stay in a *ryokan*?

Shinkansen

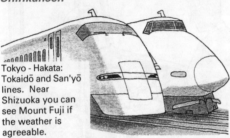

Tokyo - Morioka: Tōhoku line. Has a snow plow at the front for winter.

Tokyo - Hakata: Tokaidō and San'yō lines. Near Shizuoka you can see Mount Fuji if the weather is agreeable.

Tokyo - Niigata: Jōetsu line.

Tokyo - Nagano: Nagano line.

For long distances, Japan Railways' (JR) Shinkansen is ideal. There are five lines in operation.

Tokyo - Izu Peninsula: The Odoriko

Osaka/Tokyo - Sapporo: The Hokutosei

Special express trains

JR has a number of fast luxury trains running on its regular lines. Night trains running between Tokyo (Ueno)/Osaka and Sapporo have comfortable sleeping cars. They are so popular it might be hard to get a ticket.

Masu-no-sushi Bentō (Toyama, Hokuriku line)

Tōgé-no-Kama-meshi Bentō (Yokokawa, Shin-etsu line)

Hōbazushi Bentō (Takayama, Takayama line)

If you use JR for long distance travel, why not buy a *bentō* (lunch box) sold on many platforms throughout the country?

Each area of Japan has its own distinctive *bentō,* so you'll enjoy the variety.

coffee beer
juice
frozen *mikan* tea
shredded dried squid
peanuts
sembei crackers
local souvenirs
bentō magazines
newspapers

Refreshments on board

Shinkansen and special express trains have carts, and attendants often pass by with refreshments for sale.

Ryokan

Japanese people are losing touch with their past. But the days of yesteryear can be relived in a Japanese inn. Most *ryokan* are old-fashioned wooden buildings, though modern culture is slowly penetrating in some cases. (For example, a souvenir counter and a computer game room. These exceptions somehow contradict the true *ryokan* atmosphere.)

The *tokonoma* is a small alcove for cultural objects, like a hanging scroll and *ikebana* arrangement.

Make sure you are completely clean, and rinse off all the soap, before you enter the bath.

You will sleep on a *futon* laid on the *tatami* floor.

Usually the meal will be brought to your room.

Many *ryokan* are located in hot spring towns, in which case the baths (two large pools, one for each sex) might be crowded. There may even be an outdoor pool—the steam wafting up in winter is unforgettable.

Room charge includes a more than ample supper, and breakfast.

Seeing the Sights

Japan is a varied country, an arc of islands stretched from north to south, a mixture of old culture and new vitality. Major tourist centers are sure to have a *ryokan* that will add to your memories.

Mountains occupy much of the Japan. Lots of paths to hike through beautiful nature, volcanoes to awe you, hot springs to bathe in...

The sea is never far away, for fishing or, in certain areas, to watch pearl diving.

At many places you will have to take your shoes off before entering.

Japan's cultural history is well preserved in temples and shrines. The more famous buildings have English pamphlets.

When Japanese families travel they buy souvenirs, local products, postcards and so on. Everyone is expected to bring back something for friends and colleagues.

古典芸能を観賞する

Once you get to know a Japanese family, they may suggest you go with them to a traditional theatrical performance. Nowadays Japanese people themselves know little of this part of their own culture, so they will learn with you.

Kabuki

This unique dramatic art form developed during the *Edo* period (1615-1867), so most stories depict this era. Males play all roles, even those of women. You will enjoy the gorgeous costumes, stage sets showing ancient Japan, and stylized mannerisms. Many plays offer a unique form of music and dance.

The *Kabuki* stage

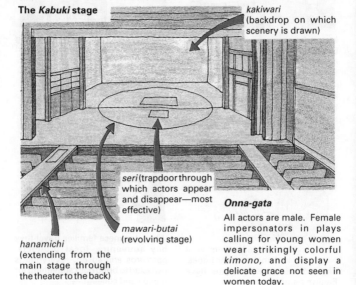

kakiwari
(backdrop on which scenery is drawn)

seri (trapdoor through which actors appear and disappear—most effective)

mawari-butai
(revolving stage)

hanamichi
(extending from the main stage through the theater to the back)

Onna-gata

All actors are male. Female impersonators in plays calling for young women wear strikingly colorful *kimono,* and display a delicate grace not seen in women today.

Some of the plays

Actors are born into the profession, and pass on their art to their sons. The *Ichikawa*s are the most well-known acting family (practically a dynasty). *Kabuki* plays are divided into *jidai-mono* (historical plays showing feudal society), *sewa-mono* (domestic plays showing townspeople), and *shosagoto* (dance pieces).

Shibaraku

A *jidai-mono* first performed in 1697. The good guys are about to be executed. A huge brave fellow shouting *"Shibaraku!"* ('One moment there!') appears and does the obvious.

Sukeroku

Another *jidai-mono* (1713). *Sukeroku* is a hero who helps the weak and punishes the wicked. Actually a *samurai* in disguise, he is known in the pleasure quarters as a chivalrous commoner. The sets and beautiful femininity are from another world.

Musumé Dōjōji

At a temple called *Dōjō-ji*, a huge bell is to be dedicated. A beautiful maiden asks to be part of the ceremony—but this temple is out of bounds to women. She gains admission on the condition that she dance. And dance she does, toward the bell under which the man (a monk) who jilted her is hiding. Then, she turns into a snake. See the ending for yourself.

Kagami-jishi

A fantasy *shosagoto* dance piece. A young woman dances with the puppet head of a lion. But the lion's spirit possesses her. She becomes the lion, and her dance becomes ferocious. The lion twirls its tremendously long mane at the climax.

Noh and *Kyōgen*

Noh and *Kyōgen* are truly ancient dramatic forms, their roots going back at least as far as the 14th century. *Noh* performance depends on subtleties and symbolism, so you should try to read the scenario before going.

Kagami-ita (decorated acoustic back-board)

Atoza (rear stage)

Hashi-gakari (bridge)

Butai (main stage)

The stage
Noh and *Kyōgen* use the same stage.

Ko-omoté

Han'nya

Ko-beshimi

Noh masks

Noh plays have two main characters, the protagonist (*shité*) and the supporting actor (*waki*). Usually only the *shité* wears a mask. With it he can portray a wide range of characters, such as a woman, old man, god, devil, or spirit. The mask, instead of hiding feelings, can help you feel the full gamut of human emotions.

Kyōgen

Kyōgen makes free use of song and dance. It is often performed between Noh plays to provide comic relief.

134

Bunraku

Bunraku is a combination of two dramatic art forms: *ayatsuri* (puppetry) and *jōruri* (dramatic chanting of a story, accompanied by music). The performances are considered to be culture at its most refined.

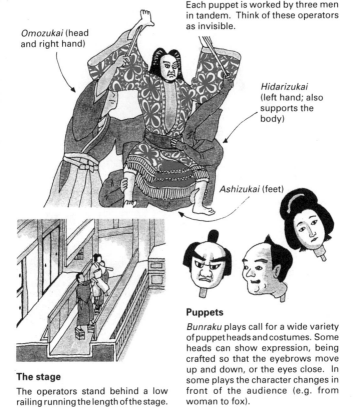

Each puppet is worked by three men in tandem. Think of these operators as invisible.

Omozukai (head and right hand)

Hidarizukai (left hand; also supports the body)

Ashizukai (feet)

The stage

The operators stand behind a low railing running the length of the stage.

Puppets

Bunraku plays call for a wide variety of puppet heads and costumes. Some heads can show expression, being crafted so that the eyebrows move up and down, or the eyes close. In some plays the character changes in front of the audience (e.g. from woman to fox).

Boys like nothing better than for Dad to take them to a game. Baseball has been the number-one game in Japan for a long time, but *sumō* and soccer are also so popular it might be hard to get tickets.

Baseball

Once you are in the spirit of things, you might find yourself buying megaphones, hats, *hachimaki* head bands...

You can buy refreshments, even beer, during the game.

Each team has its own enthusiastic supporters. Trumpeting, twirling parasols, dancing, revelry—in all the fun, men's stress levels go way down.

Sumō

Sumō, Japan's national sport, may have its origins in antiquity, but it is followed avidly today by millions. Wrestlers (called *rikishi*), each wearing only a *mawashi* loincloth, make the best use of their powerful weight on a raised earthen ring (*dohyō*).

The *dohyō-iri* ceremony, "entering the ring," is performed by wrestlers of *makuuchi* rank before the matches begin. Their colorful *keshō-mawashi*, each one different, make quite a sight.

A great place to watch *sumō* is a special boxed-in seat (*masu-seki*) with room for about four people. But demand for these seats is high.

Before the match, the *rikishi* throw salt on the *dohyō*. This ritual is to purify the earth upon which they might fall in a few moments.

The costume of the referee (*gyōji*) will tell you his rank—the more elaborate it is, the higher his rank. It is the *gyōji*'s job to name the winner. Winning is very simple: push any part of the opponent out of the ring, or get any part of his body (except the soles of the feet) to touch the ground in the ring.

Soccer

From the day of its inception in 1993, Japan's professional soccer league (J. League) has had a tremendous following, especially among the young (even the very young). Fans, some wearing the hats and uniforms of their favorite team, or with faces painted in their team's colors, go crazy at games.

J1 League, composed of 16 teams, imports talent from overseas. All of the League's players are true professionals.

Tickets might be hard to get—demand is heavy, and stadiums are smaller than those for baseball.

Baseball fans play trumpets and beat drums. Soccer fanatics show their passion with megaphones and flags.

School Sports Day

Baseball for grown men, soccer for the young. But for parents of young children, School Sports Day, held annually in autumn, comes before anything else. These meets always fall on a Sunday so that parents can attend.

Students practice for a month before the event. It is their teachers' job to make sure everyone is in top shape and can march in unison in the parade. Cheerleader groups practice too, and prepare props such as flags.

Everything begins with fireworks. Students are divided into two groups, red and white (with caps colored accordingly). There are all kinds of competitions, such as races, a mock cavalry battle, and artistic dancing, but the main event is undoubtedly the relay race.

Parents have eyes mainly on their kids, when they aren't adjusting their video cameras.

Mothers and fathers also get into the act too for one event, often the tug-of-war. In their zeal to perform well in front of their kids, some out-of-shape parents end up with aches, bruises, or worse.

KARAOKÉ

カラオケ

Karaoké started in bars in the 1970s, but has spread to homes for family sessions as well. Music is recorded on tape, CD or laser disc —but the singing you do yourself.

Karaoké is one of Japan's most popular leisure activities. It goes well with a drink, which is perhaps why pubs have the equipment and staff (including a young woman who needs a partner for a duet) to sing.

But the staff knows you need an audience, so they may oblige by beating time by hand or with a tambourine.

The more songs you sing, the higher the charge.

The laser disc provides the music, video scenes that fit the song, and the lyrics in sub-title form at the bottom of the screen. Sing the word that is indicated by the changing color, and you can't go wrong.

People are so busy getting ready for their own performances that perhaps few are listening to yours.

Karaoké equipment in the home can disturb the neighbors, so when you want to belt it out it's better to go elsewhere. Big business has found a niche here —the *karaoké* box. These are sound-insulated rooms in large buildings, conveniently located for car or train travel.

Charges are calculated by the hour, so a family outing can be quite reasonable.

Let's look through the glass window of the sound-proof door. Comfortable seats, the latest equipment (operated by remote control), the ideal atmosphere to get rid of all that built-up stress.

Karaoké boxes are popular among high-school students too, and parents cannot complain because no alcohol is served.

Some of the songs are in English, so give it a try if you have a chance. In Japan, whether you can carry a tune or not is irrelevant to having a good time.

INDOOR GAMES

ゲームをする

Games bring a family together. And it's a good way to break the ice, so when you visit someone, why not suggest a game?

Go, shōgi and mah-jongg were imported from China, and now have many avid Japanese players, some professional. From the West have come card games, including Uno.

Go

Black has 181 stones, white 180 (black plays first). Stones are kept in a *goké,* which is a round, covered container made of mulberry or cherry wood.

The board has 19 vertical and 19 horizontal lines (and therefore 361 intersections). Each leg is shaped like a gardenia nut.

Two players sit on opposite sides of a board made of nutmeg or ginko wood.

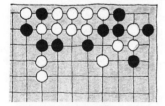

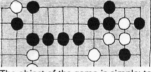

Players take turns placing their stones on unoccupied intersections. Stones cannot be removed once played, unless they are captured (i.e., when surrounded by the opponent, with no empty spaces remaining within the enclosure).

The object of the game is simple: to surround and protect as much territory as possible. When all stones have been played, or nothing further can be done, captured stones are placed in the opponent's vacant spaces. The winner is the one controlling the greater number of empty intersections (in this case, black has 8 points).

142

Shōgi

Both chess and *shōgi* originated in India, so it is natural they should be similar (though the *shōgi* board has 9 squares to a side). The object is the same: to checkmate the opponent's king.

Specific rules apply to the movement of each piece, again, as in chess.

Enemy territory

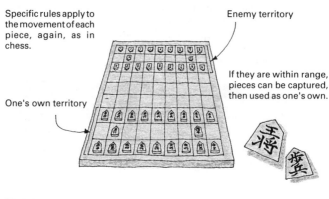

If they are within range, pieces can be captured, then used as one's own.

One's own territory

Mah-jong

Mah-jong (even the name comes from China) is somewhat like rummy, the object being to collect sets and sequences. But instead of 52 cards, the game uses 136 small colorful tiles.

Usually four people play, and money often changes hands. Mah-jong parlors have become very popular since World War II.

Camaraderie among men is important for the workplace. Since things can get up-tight and stressful during the day, drinking after work is a good way to keep relationships on an even keel. If superiors or colleagues suggest you go drinking with them—and they will—it is pretty hard to refuse.

This gesture means, "Let's go for a drink (or two)." To make it, pretend you are about to drink from a small *saké* cup.

The majority of drinking establishments are small bars with a working-class atmosphere. *'Aka-chōchin'* ('red lantern') bars are a good example. Look for the inevitable red lantern hanging outside.

Do not pour your own drink. Pour his for him, and he will return the favor. Now the day's stress disappears, and real feelings surface.

Something light but nutritious comes with the alcohol. Often drinkers have this instead of supper, then grab a bite on the way home.

Outside the cabaret is a *"yobi-komi,"* who claps his hands and invites you inside with a loud cheerful voice.

Cabarets

Quite a few steps up the social ladder from the *aka-chōchin* is the cabaret. A hostess will pour the alcohol and drink (or rather, sip) with you. Almost all of the guests are male.

Nightclubs

Higher up in scale, above the cabaret, is the nightclub. It is more expensive, but good for entertaining important guests. The women are witty, charming, and each more beautiful than the next.

Some drinking establishments are often concentrated in the same area, thereby creating a distinctive atmosphere. Two famous Tokyo drinking districts are Akasaka and Kabuki-chō. The men in black bow-ties are *yobi-komi.*

Japanese men, unfortunately, hold their liquor poorly. Some run into difficulties on the way home.

WHEN DAD HAS TIME FOR THE KIDS
子どもとつきあう

With his job, overtime and drinking with fellow workers, Dad has little time left over for his family. But when he does, there are all kinds of places to take the kids to.

Amusement parks
Trying to get there by car may not be good for Dad's blood pressure—it is far better (and faster) to take the train or bus.

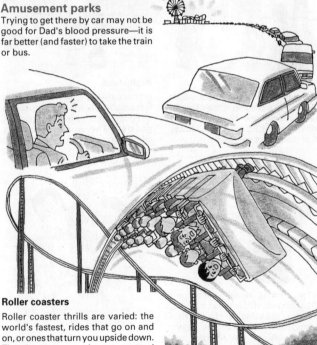

Roller coasters
Roller coaster thrills are varied: the world's fastest, rides that go on and on, or ones that turn you upside down. There's even one where you stand rather than sit.

Zoos

All kids like a zoo, and for Dad it's cheaper than an amusement park. Ueno Zoo in Tokyo is famous for its pandas. (If you have a picnic, you won't want to be downwind from the cages.)

Computer game centers

One way Dad can relate to the kids is by taking them to a high-tech computer game center—each game costs from 100 to 200 yen.

Theme Parks

Japan has adopted the American invention, the theme park. Nagasaki Prefecture has created a fantasy-land called Huis Ten Bosch, the theme being Holland: canals, reproductions of old buildings, and formal gardens. You can stay the night in a hotel here.

But parks are a lot cheaper, and provide good exercise.

Anyone hit is out of the game.

Dodgeball

Divide into two teams on a square piece of ground. Throw the ball at someone on the opposite team.

THE MOTHER: ANCHOR FOR THE ENTIRE FAMILY

奥さんにつきあう

With Dad at work, and the kids at school or *juku*, even in these days of liberation it is the mother who is left with the shopping to do. But since it is she who controls the family's budget (even Dad only gets an allowance from her), she is a very perceptive shopper.

Shopping
Shopping with the family, though not often possible, is one pleasure women enjoy.

Bills and coins

¥1,000   ¥2,000   ¥5,000   ¥10,000

¥1   ¥5   ¥10   ¥50   ¥100   ¥500

Credit cards are common, but cash is still used for most purchases. Cash dispensers are now indispensable when setting out for the day's shopping.

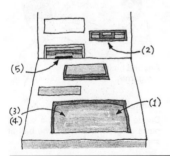

How to withdraw money from an ATM:

(1) Choose the function (in this case 'withdrawal;' some other functions are deposit and transfer).
(2) Insert your cash card.
(3) Input your personal number.
(4) Input the amount you need.
(5) Pull out the card and money (some machines give coins as well).

Most department stores are open from 10:00 am to 7:00 pm. Department stores are open on Sundays and holidays (the best days for shopping), and closed one day during the week. You will probably be welcomed to the store with a bow and a smile.

A uniformed elevator operator will get you to the floor you want.

Department stores hold special sales (30 to 50% off) at the beginning of January and August. Housewives seem to have an innate ability to squeeze through the crowds on these days.

You may have lunch (quite reasonably priced) on the top floor of the department store. The choice is varied: Japanese, Chinese, or Western.

Fresh fish are cleaned and prepared in front of you.

Groceries for supper are quite expensive at department stores, so you will probably buy food near home. Large supermarkets near the station have everything you could possibly need.

If you know the shopkeeper, you may get a slight discount (though in Japan it is bad form to bargain).

Shopping is hard work, and lugging everything home is physical labor.

FROM THE STONE AGE TO THE AGE OF AFFLUENCE

家族の変遷

原始・古代

From the Stone Age to the Introduction of Agriculture

Thousands of years ago, before rice was cultivated in Japan, the ancestors of today's Japanese lived by hunting and gathering. Life was probably nomadic at first, but in time small settlements sprang up on the highlands and beside the sea.

Pit dwellings

Single families (what we would call nuclear families), each with about six or seven members, lived in simple pit dwellings. Villagers were typically related to each other.

Polygamy

Scholars suggest that in those days one man might have been allowed several wives.

Was society matrilineal or patrilineal?

Although some anthropologists state that Japanese society was always patrilineal, others insist that at one time lineage was determined through the mother. They support their argument with the examples of the Sun Goddess *Amaterasu Ōmikami*, who is regarded as having started the imperial line, and Himiko, a queen who led the Japanese federation in the third century A.D.

From the Beginning of Agriculture to the Rise of Military Government

Rice cultivation was introduced into Japan from the continent about 2000 years ago. Villages then naturally sprang up on flat lowlands and the surrounding hills. Agriculture allowed some families to accumulate wealth in the form of land and grain. Power became centralized, and a system of taxation (demanding either produce or labor) was introduced.

"Marriage" in those days

Love and marriage were not compartmentalized as they are today—a man would simply visit a woman frequently for a mutually advantageous period of time. During this time society at large would recognize them as a "married couple."

Equality between the sexes

Women, like men, could inherit property. In other ways too society placed men and women on an equal footing. Many of the famous writers of the time were women.

Polyandry and polygamy

In those days, some women took several men as their husbands, just as some men were polygamous.

THE MEDIEVAL PERIOD
(12th to 16th Centuries)
中世＜12〜16世紀＞

The golden age of the aristocracy (10th and 11th centuries) gave way to military might. The warrior class, for its own reasons, made "*ié*" a fundamental principle of society. *Ié* is the family household, the ideal being that one's lineage continues unbroken from one generation to the next. During this period, power within the family became concentrated in the hands of the patriarch or father.

Lineage traced through the oldest son

In the 13th and 14th centuries it became common for the oldest son to inherit the family's property and the title of head of the household. This system filtered down to all social strata, and remains an important factor in Japanese society today.

Rights and responsibilities of the patriarch

In addition to inheriting the household property, the eldest son wielded considerable authority over the very future of his family.

(1) The right to name the next head of the household (who would later inherit the family estate and become the next family autocrat).

(2) The right to eject, unilaterally and completely, any member of the family from the household.

(3) The right to control and administer the family estate as he saw fit.

154

Why was the eldest son so privileged?

At one time, all sons inherited property upon their parents' death. But this led to frequent squabbles over the estate. Naming one person the sole beneficiary was a way to avoid these unseemly disputes.

Monogamy

To ensure a continual family line, it was necessary to adopt monogamy. Monogamy brought with it the ritual of the marriage ceremony and the stigma of a wife's adultery.

Forming a new family and a new household

Before the rise in influence of the *samurai* class, a man would just move in with a woman, thereby starting a family. The *ié* system changed social norms—a young couple was now expected to marry formally, then set up a new and stable household.

Commoners

With the exception of the warrior and aristocratic classes, most people led simple, even poor lives. These peasants, living in units of five or six to a family, were often dirt-poor. Some, though, could afford to employ others to help work the fields.

Heaven help those not born the eldest son

In *samurai* families it was the eldest son who had sole right to inherit property. This norm was adopted slowly by all classes of Japanese society. Female offspring were excluded first, then all boys, except the eldest, were ignored as well. Daughters would eventually marry (thereby leaving the family), but all sons except the first-born might be doomed to bachelorhood, eking out a living as manual laborers for their eldest brother.

Pecking order

Old Japanese houses, whether built for *samurai* or peasants, were constructed with a homey room with a sunken hearth. This was essentially a fireplace, called an *irori*, and was the main source of warmth in winter, an ideal place for the entire family to congregate for meals and get-togethers. Each person had a specific place to sit, depending upon rank within the family.

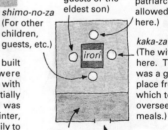

kyaku-za (Reserved for guests or the eldest son)

yoko-za (Only the patriarch was allowed to sit here.)

shimo-no-za (For other children, guests, etc.)

kaka-za (The wife sat here. This was a good place from which to oversee meals.)

doma (Room with packed-earth floor)

entrance

Position of Women in Japanese Society, Past and Present

With the advent of a society centered on the military, the place of women sank lower and lower.

From the 12th to the 18th centuries, women could not become head of the family household. In many cases, especially in *samurai* families, the wife was expected to bear a son at all costs. Otherwise, the couple was presented with two unattractive alternatives: adoption of a male heir, or the end of the family line.

Two Japanese expressions show how men were regarded as the center of society. When a woman married she was said to *"yomé ni hairu"* (enter another house as a wife); when a man married he was said to *"yomé o toru"* (take possession of a wife).

Women could play no official role in the Imperial Court or military government. The only exceptions were ladies-in-waiting.

A woman's role in society was twofold: to support her husband and to bring up the children.

THE RECENT PAST

The *Edo* Period (1615 - 1867)

Tokugawa Ieyasu's Shogunate unified and pacified Japan, but put the entire country under the control of the military. The idea of *"ié"* (a household's lineage being traced through the male line) was made the norm throughout Japan. Social order was characterized by the feudal concept of lord and vassal: under the *Shōgun* were sworn vassals, the *daimyō* and *samurai*. Peasants were located far down the scale, near the bottom.

Importance of the *"ié"* system

Under the military class the *ié* system became the basic framework of society. The system established social status, and status, for its part, helped to determine social advancement within the system.

Peace and security in return for allegiance

Samurai served their *daimyō,* and in so doing gave their unswerving allegiance to the *Shōgun* (which meant being prepared to fight, even die, for him). In return, the *daimyō* granted land or rice to their *samurai,* and guaranteed peace and security to their families.

peace and security for the household

allegiance

Rights and responsibilities

The *daimyō* granted land or rice to their *samurai*, i.e., to the head of the *samurai* household. This right to *daimyō* favor was inherited by the heir upon the death of the old *samurai*. For this reason, the very future of an entire *samurai* household was in the hands of its head (almost always the eldest son).

Family crests

Although it is true that some families suffered the ignominy of dissolution, ideally the family had its roots in the distant past, and would continue indefinitely into the future. Families had an identity, an existence, of their own. The family crest symbolized this identity. Here are some examples of family crests.

Concubines

During this feudal period, highly placed men, including the *Shōgun* himself, were free to bring a concubine (perhaps more than one) into their household. This was a kind of insurance policy—if the wife could not produce a male heir, the family line would continue through a son sired with another woman.

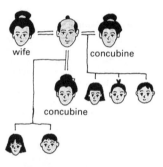

Family motto

In addition to the crest, a family motto, too, was passed down from one generation to the next. The motto stated an ethical principle which was to guide the entire family. The contemporary Japanese company (in a sense, a large family) has adopted this same practice.

Samurai family mottoes
- Respect and honor your ancestors →
- Work together harmoniously for your family's prosperity →
- Apply yourself to martial arts, and cultivate the faithful, virtuous heart of a true *samurai* →
- Live simply and economically →

Modern company mottoes
- Work hard and respect the company founder's ideals
- Work together harmoniously for your company's prosperity
- Apply yourself diligently to your job, and show fidelity to your company
- Cut costs to the bone, and strive for greater profits

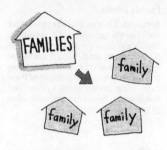

和　勤勉　倹約

The peasant family

In the early part of the *Edo* period (1615-1867), peasant households often included the families of younger brothers and other relatives. But by mid-*Edo* the *samurai* concept of family inheritance had spread to this class too—younger brothers left the family hearth, and daughters married out of the family.

The peasant ideal: stability

The peasant family, in its adoption of the *ié* system, embraced other *samurai* ideals, too: peaceful stability, diligence and frugality. Any family member who jeopardized the household's stability could be disowned (if a son or daughter) or divorced (if a wife).

Children regarded as "treasure"

Children were security for one's old age and a guarantee that the family would continue. Beginning in the 18th century, children were sent to *terakoya* schools to learn reading, writing and the abacus.

Destitute peasants

Some peasants, especially in times of economic decline, were so poor that an extra child was anything but a treasure. In extreme cases this could lead to the terrible practice of *mabiki* (literally thinning out, i.e. infanticide).

Ancient Dwelling for the Extended Family

Deep in the mountains of Gifu prefecture, in a village called Shirakawa, are a group of unusual farmhouses constructed in the *gasshō-zukuri* style of the mid-*Edo* period. According to a survey done in 1876, on average each dwelling housed an extended family of 16 persons. Since farmland in the mountains was too scarce to divide up into smaller lots, houses became bigger instead.

Outside, the houses are truly beautiful. Inside they are huge, divided into four or five stories.

The ground floor plan of one house:

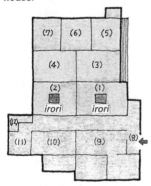

Even the design of the house shows the respect and honor shown the head of the house-hold and his eldest son.

(1) Room to receive guests
(2) Dining room. Cooking usually done at the *irori*.
(3) Bedroom for eldest son or important guest
(4) Room for the women (wives and daughters), and also for a retired family head
(5) Room with Buddhist family altar
(6) Guest bedroom
(7) Bedroom for the family head. The only room reserved for one person.
(8) Entrance
(9) Stable for horses. Other sons slept immediately above here.
(10) Room for farm work
(11) Kitchen
(12) Bath

With the collapse of military government in 1867, Japan became a modern state unified under the Emperor. Society's foundations were shaken. The family system was not immune to change either: with the emergence of a nationalistic, militaristic state, authoritarian patriarchal figures and a family centered around males continued to be the social norm.

For the nation and for glory

Under the slogan, "national prosperity and military strength," the government decided to bureaucratically administer the *ié* system. The names of all people in all households were recorded in family registers. This made conscription and taxation easy.

Equality on paper only

Feudalism had divided society into four classes: the warrior class, peasants, artisans and merchants. Modernization swept away this system, enabling people, in theory, complete freedom to marry and choose a profession. But in actual fact the former warrior class continued to enjoy special privileges, and the lowly citizen was hardly more respected than before.

The *Meiji* Constitution

The now-abandoned Constitution of the Empire of Japan (1889) stated that Japan was to be reigned over by the unbroken line of Emperors. The implication here was that the *ié* household system was to foster obedience to the Emperor (in other words, the State).

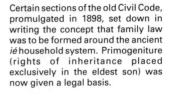

Certain sections of the old Civil Code, promulgated in 1898, set down in writing the concept that family law was to be formed around the ancient *ié* household system. Primogeniture (rights of inheritance placed exclusively in the eldest son) was now given a legal basis.

Comparison of past and present civil codes

Old Civil Code
- The head of household was given → great authority over family affairs.
- Men under 30 and women under → 25 could not marry without their parents' consent.
- A wife was required to assume her → husband's family name.
- The husband had the right to control → and administer his wife's property.

Civil Code Now In Effect
- No mention of authority
- Men 18 or over, and women 16 or over, can legally marry (but parents' consent is needed for those under 20).
- One spouse is to assume the family name of the other.
- Husband and wife have equal property rights.

Vertical family relationships

The old Civil Code was based on the assumption that the eldest son would inherit the family estate. Family relationships were oriented vertically (parent to child) rather than horizontally (husband and wife, and siblings with equal rights). Family members at the lower end of the vertical axis were expected to honor and respect those above. In the *Meiji* period the wife's role was to serve her husband and his parents, while the children were expected to show filial piety.

Families in the *Meiji* period

The westernization of Japan brought dependence upon the convenience of gas and electricity. But family life, though modern in this respect, was not alienated as it often is today—on the contrary, family members had very little privacy, and considered themselves a strongly-knit group.

Shimazaki Tōson —Writer
Shimazaki has left us with this thought: "Unless the *ié* system is destroyed, the individual will never be truly free."

Hiratsuka Raichō —Feminist
This controversial social activist is known for not registering her marriage, indeed calling her marriage a "joint living arrangement."

Taishō democracy

After the demise of the Emperor Meiji came the *Taishō* period (1912-1926). Around this time a popular movement, partly led by the intellectual elite, arose to sweep away old restrictions and to introduce true democracy, a democracy that would encompass greater freedom within the family. But this movement was swept aside by the stronger forces of militarism.

Towards war

After the beginning of the *Shōwa* period in 1926, the *ié* system became more and more important as a pillar of the nationalistic and militaristic state. The government promulgated the idea that citizens were the children of the Emperor. To strengthen the country militarily, couples were strongly urged to have many children—mothers with 10 children were by no means uncommon.

(At the family level)

Parent
|
Child

=

(At the nation-state level)

Emperor
|
All citizens

Looking at the Family through Proverbs

Oya kōkō o shitai toki ni oya wa nashi

By the time you realize your parents' virtues, they are no longer alive to receive your thanks. (The moral is, of course, to treat your parents well while you have the chance.)

Oya no iken to hiyazaké wa atodé kiku

Just as it takes time for cold *saké* to make you pleasantly mellow, so too will you realize your parents' wisdom only at a later date.

Oya wa naku-tomo ko wa sodatsu

Children grow up well even without their parents. (This maxim states that society is more caring than it may appear.)

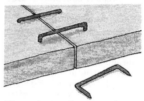

Ko wa kasugai

Children are the glue that keep a couple together.

Kawaii ko ni-wa tabi o saseyo

Let your child learn hardship for his own good.

Onna, sankai ni ié nashi

A woman's fate is to be dependent three times (upon her parents when young, upon her husband when grown, and upon her children when old).

With military defeat and ruination in 1945, many Japanese social values were turned upside down. The family, previously forced to accommodate itself to the nation-state, suddenly found itself confronted with a new concept: freedom of the individual. The negative side to this great change was the weakening of bonds that had kept the family a closely-knit unit.

The post-war constitution

One year after the end of the war Japan's present constitution was promulgated. Enshrined therein are three ideals: sovereignty resides with the people; fundamental human rights; and renunciation of war. The Emperor is described as a symbol of the state and the unity of the people. The individual is accorded every respect, and women and men are accorded equality. Article 24 refers explicitly to the "equal rights of husband and wife."

The new Civil Code

The new Civil Code, promulgated in 1947, eliminated the legal basis of the *ié* system and abolished a wife's subordination. Couples became free to marry and divorce, both gained equal rights and responsibilities vis-a-vis their children, and rights to inheritance were made equal. The household register system was also changed, fixing the household unit as a married couple and their unmarried children, or as an individual with or without children.

The end of feudalistic influences

In addition, the new Civil Code abolished the special rights of the head of the household, rights that had existed since the days of the feudal warrior. But tradition does live on: the family head (the husband, the father) is still held up as a figure to be respected.

Alienation within the family

With the abandonment of the *ié* system and the influence of modern individualism, the bonds holding the family together have stretched thinner and thinner. The mass adoption of television sets around 1960 have reduced the opportunities for communication between husband and wife or parents and children.

Unbelievably low birthrate

The nuclear family is the norm today. On the average, a woman gives birth to only about 1.8 children during her lifetime. Reasons given for this extremely low level are the expense of raising and educating a child, and the wife's desire to work.

The nuclear family

Since World War II, the nuclear family has become the rule. Once they are old enough, children, even the eldest son, leave the family nest to start their own individual households.

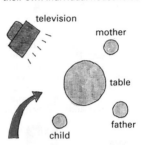

television

mother

table

father

child

Television and seating arrangement

In ancient days the head of the household sat in the place of honor near the *irori*. The *irori* has become a TV, but otherwise things have changed little.

Women's independence

The post-war woman has certainly come a long way—a job (full- or part-time), volunteer work, holding her own in society. The pre-war generation is undoubtedly aghast at the number of women who turn their noses up at the very idea of marriage.

Looking at the Contemporary Family through Modern Expressions

Kagikko

The English expression here is "latchkey kid." This saying sprang up in the 1960s, when many children began to take the house key to school, because they would later come home to an empty house (Mom and Dad being at work).

Meshi, kané, urusē

Since their fathers are always away at work (or otherwise occupied), communication between father and child (especially son) breaks down. All the father hears from his boy is *"Meshi!"* ("I'm hungry!"), *"Kané!"* ("Give me my allowance!") and *"Urusē"* ("Shut up!").

Kurenai-zoku

The many people (*zoku*) who complain about others (e.g. their spouses or parents) end the gripe with: *"... shité kurenai"* (they won't do ... for me).

My Home shugi

"My Home" is an Anglicism, expressing the desire of many men to buy and enjoy their own home. Japan's phenomenal economic growth after the war made this possible. Yet during this time a man's major concern (*shugi*) was expected to be his company, so this expression has a slight sarcastic side to it.

DINKS

The U.S. is the source of this expression: "Double Income, No Kids."

Hotaru-zoku

Fathers in this group (*zoku*) are those who are forced outside at night to enjoy a cigarette. The red cigarette moving about in the dark looks like a firefly (*hotaru*).

CHAPTER 6

FAMILY PROBLEMS
家族の問題

STRESS

ストレス

"Home Sweet Home" is the ideal, but not always the reality. Families face a number of social pressures. The resulting stress manifests itself in minor, sometimes major problems.

What the husband and father feels:

Bosses and clients make a lot of demands, and somehow he brings all of the stress home with him.

Finally he retires. His work was his life, so now he has nothing to live for.

What the wife and mother feels:

Housework, bringing up children, looking after hubby... Stress leads to resentment.

Alone from morning to night... Solitude leads to depression.

What the child feels:

Examination hell can lead to a refusal to go to school. And this can lead to violence in the home.

Parents expect too much.

What the elderly feel:

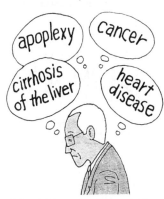

Old and sick, getting older and sicker.

Will our kids look after us until we die?

EDUCATION BLUES

教育問題

More than 90% of Japanese junior high graduates go on to senior high school. Japanese society still judges one by the school one has attended. To get into a good senior high school (and later, into university) students must go through "examination hell," which can be as hard on the parents as on their kids.

Scholastic performance is judged only through testing, the results of which are cold figures comparing each student against a norm. It is now generally accepted that this 'hensachi' system lacks relevance, but fundamental improvements are not off the drawing board.

Some students refuse to go to school, and will not even say why. More senior high students are quitting too.

"Ijimé" is another social problem. A number of pupils will tease, taunt and bully someone they feel deserves it. This has even led to suicide or, on rare occasions, accidental (?) death.

The curriculum is followed to the letter, learning is by rote, students are strictly controlled by teachers. Under this system individuality has little chance to develop.

172

Continual studying for exams leads to stress. Students might take it out on their parents, school, or society in general.

Violence in the home

Motorcycle gangs

Shoplifting

Glue sniffing

Social skills, ethical behavior, and becoming a cooperative member of society are essential, yet some parents ignore everything except the question, "Are they studying hard?"

Teachers know cramming knowledge into young heads is not everything. In 1992 schools started relaxing things a little, by taking two Saturdays off a month.

WHERE'S DAD?

父親の不在

Since World War II, and especially since the beginning of Japan's tremendous economic growth, the father's presence in the home has greatly diminished. Men are part of an army of company workers, on campaigns away from home.

Long working hours are followed by drinking bouts with fellow workers, or by entertaining clients. Dad often arrives home late at night, with only sleep on his mind.

The fate for some is 'karōshi'—death from overwork.

Another possibility, not so extreme, is a posting far away. The wife and kids often stay behind.

Yet another possible fate is the impression one is not wanted at home—this can lead to sorrows drowned in alcohol, alone every evening in some bar.

At the end of the company road is retirement, with no idea of what to do at home. This does nothing for self-esteem.

The type of family where the father is rarely at home can result in selfish children too dependent on their mothers.

Many fathers eat supper with the family only once or twice a week.

One advantage of a recession is less overtime. The negative trends described above are beginning to reverse themselves.

Japanese men have long been known for the three weaknesses listed above. In these modern times husbands and fathers tempted down one of these paths may find a broken home at the end of it.

The Japanese see nothing wrong with a few drinks after work or at home. But some men cannot survive without the bottle, and for a few, drunkenness results in violence in the home.

Alcoholism can lead to divorce. "I would still love him, if it hadn't been for his drinking," is an all too familiar refrain sung by divorcees.

Society has also turned a critical eye on the "kitchen drinker," the woman alone in the home, dependent on booze.

There are lots of places to satisfy the male urge to gamble, especially the races (horses, bicycles and speedboats). Some husbands cover their losses with household savings, then fall deeper and deeper into the red.

Tabloids have a field day covering compulsive gamblers who, after suffering huge losses, steal money or kidnap someone for ransom.

And then there is the third vice: the other woman, often a nightclub hostess who needs lots of money to keep the relationship off rocky ground. The wife, in charge of money matters, is never amused if (or when) she finds out.

A word often bandied about these days is *"furin,"* (unethical behavior, i.e. cheating on one's spouse). The workplace for some reason is a convenient place to start a clandestine relationship; when the cat is out of the bag, a man might lose both his job and his family.

A man would find his wife's *furin* beyond the pale. But he might consider his own sleeping around of little consequence, since he remains deeply attached to his wife. In the past this *"uwaki"* was usually winked at by society, while the wife used to make an attempt to ignore it.

When discussing problems the modern Japanese family faces, near the top of the list is housing. City land is so expensive that buying a house in a convenient area is practically out of the question, unless one is rich. For many people the solution is to go deep into debt, and live far from work.

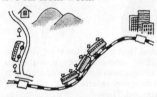

Many company employees work near the city center and reside at least 50 km away. Hours commuting on the train every day are extra hours spent away from home. This is another reason why family members drift apart from each other.

Some years ago the European media referred to Japanese houses as "rabbit hutches" (usagi-goya). An apt description, considering the average area of a Tokyo dwelling is a mere 60m². And the hutches show little sign of becoming less cramped.

The one-room condo

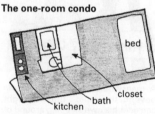

bed

closet

bath

kitchen

Nowadays many young urban residents live alone in a six-mat room (about 10 m²) with kitchen, toilet and bath. The "one room condo" boasts a total area of about 20 m².

With exorbitant prices the only answer is to tie oneself into a long-term loan. Long-term here could very well mean your whole life, plus part of your children's.

Large apartment blocks and high-rises provide kids with another excuse to stay indoors, and lead to urban isolation.

For those who can afford it, the trend is towards separate rooms for each person. This can result in family members becoming distant from each other.

Low birth rates and high housing costs are cutting back on the prevalence of the nuclear family: even after a child's marriage the young couple may live with one set of parents.

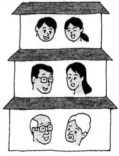

Sections of society are edging slowly back to the way it used to be—three generations under one roof. Builders recognize the trend and are constructing some houses accordingly.

MOTHER-IN-LAW PROBLEMS

嫁と姑

Weddings and honeymoons are a time of bliss, but one must always wake up to reality. For the young wife, reality means her mother-in-law (*shūtomé*).

A few years ago young women pampered themselves by naming three conditions for marriage: a house, a car, and no mother-in-law. But men today are likely to be the only son in the family, so realistic girls know a mother-in-law cannot be shunted off to bother someone else.

The typical Japanese mother devotes herself incessantly to her son, forming a seemingly exclusive bond. To the older woman, the bride has forced her way in. If things get out of hand, all three can suffer.

The character for "young wife":

YOMÉ

嫁

↑   └──┘
WOMAN   HOME

The character for "mother-in-law":

SHŪTO

姑

└──┘   ↑
WOMAN   OLD

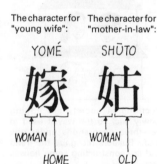

Popular television dramas often take up this theme.

The mother-in-law can find all kinds of justifications for the need to needle and torment.

That is not how to clean a house.

Let me show you how to bring up your child.

Your cooking is a disgrace.

The mother-in-law can vent her frustration in the neighborhood, where outsiders are all too willing to take her part.

Japanese society sees mother-in-law trouble as something unavoidable. It also expects the husband to jump into the fray to sort things out. But he is often torn both ways and ends up indecisive and ineffectual.

DIVORCE

離婚

In the old days it was the husband who usually demanded a divorce. But now sexual equality means equal rights in this regard, too. The availability of jobs for women is one important factor here.

1998 saw a total of 243,102 divorces in Japan (this works out to 666 each day). Until that year divorce had been on the decline for some time, so the sudden rise gave social commentators a lot to talk about.

Compared to Europe or North America, marriages in Japan break down less frequently. Yet if both partners agree to the divorce, it is probably easier in Japan than anywhere else to cut the knot. No messy court case is involved: they just register the divorce at City Hall (probably the same place where they registered their marriage).

The traditional stereotype tells of long-suffering wives enduring overbearing husbands. Those days are long gone. More often than not it is the woman who prepares the divorce paper.

A man in middle age may find this his fate, perhaps after his retirement.

Here are factors that can lead to a divorce by consent.

We just aren't suited for each other.

Another woman.

Money problems.

I can't stand the in-laws.

Honeymoons often start out from Tokyo's Narita International Airport. If a young couple marries in haste, all that time together overseas can be a rude awakening, which can lead to a so-called "*Narita Rikon*" (Narita divorce) at the airport upon return.

Years ago, remarrying invited negative comment, but that is much less the case now.

The Japanese family has changed greatly since the end of World War II. What does the future hold?

1997 census statistics tell us the average Japanese household has 2.79 people. (50 years ago it was about 5.) This reflects the low birth rate, the prevalence of nuclear families and the modern option, living alone. The figure will probably continue to drop.

The institution of marriage now offers fewer advantages. Men and women are marrying later, or not at all. And the traditional persistent social pressures on single people in their 20s and 30s are now passe.

In some countries unmarried couples can cohabit and enjoy the same legal rights as a formally married husband and wife. This type of family might one day be recognized by Japanese law too.

The Japanese Civil Code states that when a man and woman marry, one must take the family name of the other. Japan is the only country that insists one surname must be abandoned. In some circles this requirement is being questioned, and may be dropped in the future.

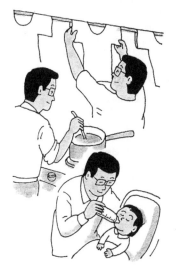

Just as women are now assuming a more active role outside the home, so too are men playing a bigger part in it. Social trends point towards men lending a hand with the housework, even taking time off work to help take care of the baby.

Japan's society is aging. Looking after the old folks is a family issue, but the government is being asked to do more too.

INDEX

F

G

Graduation trip

H

M

N

O

P

R

S

英文 日本絵とき事典
ILLUSTRATED
JAPANESE FAMILY & CULTURE

初版発行　1994年3月1日
改訂6版　2003年9月1日
　　　　　（Sep. 1. 2003 6th edition）
編 集 人　黒澤明夫
発 行 人　安斎二三夫
発 行 所　JTB
印 刷 所　JTB印刷

企画・編集　るるぶ社　海外編集局
取材・編集協力　アーバン・トランスレーション
イラスト　松下正己
表紙デザイン　東　芳純
翻　　訳　Nathan Mathews, Urban Connections

●JTB発行の図書のご注文は
出版販売センター　☎03-5796-5593
〒140-0002 東京都品川区東品川2-3-11 JTBビル7階
●本書の内容のお問合せは
るるぶ社　海外編集局　☎03-5796-5578
〒140-0002 東京都品川区東品川2-3-11 JTBビル7階
●広告のお問合せは
出版事業局 広告本部　☎03-5796-5531
●旅の完全サイト
http://rurubu.com/